American Family Farmland is required reading for anyone who will bequeath or has inherited a farm. It showcases the strength of one of our country's greatest legacies and ensures it will endure for generations to come. Johnny Klemme guides the reader through the process of preserving not only the tangible assets but also the many intangible aspects involved in safeguarding this heritage as farm ownership passes from one generation to the next. Honor, dignity, and respect are emphasized, ensuring that family values and traditions live on. In a gentle yet straightforward manner, Klemme has guided countless families through one of the most important—and often stressful—events in their history. He shares his wisdom and many insightful stories from personal experience, and his love for farming families shines through on every page.

— **DR. JASON RANDALL,** *Author, and Farmland Owner in Illinois, Indiana, & Wisconsin*

In *American Family Farmland,* Johnny gives landowners a straightforward, comprehensive, and easy-to-understand guide for protecting our most valuable assets — the family farm and the land and soil beneath it. This is a must-read for families committed to preserving their farming heritage across generations. The book thoughtfully addresses the difficult decisions involving tradition, legacy, and stewardship, highlighting Johnny's proactive and empathetic approach. Ultimately, your farm's legacy hinges on making informed, intentional choices, and Johnny expertly guides you through this journey with compassion.

— **RICK CLARK,** *Fifth Generation Farmer / Farm Green*

AMERICAN FAMILY FARMLAND

PRESERVING VALUES
AND CREATING WEALTH

AMERICAN FAMILY FARMLAND

PRESERVING VALUES

AND CREATING WEALTH

A LANDOWNERS GUIDE TO INHERITING THE FARM

JOHNNY KLEMME

Niche Pressworks
Indianapolis, IN

Cover Artwork by Michelle Darling

Published by Niche Pressworks; NichePressworks.com
Indianapolis, IN

ISBN
Hardcover: 978-1-962956-82-6
Paperback: 978-1-962956-83-3
eBook: 978-1-962956-84-0

Library of Congress Cataloging-in-Publication Data on File at lccn.loc.gov

Dedication

This book is dedicated in memory of our own family farm. To my parents, John & Linda, and my grandparents, Dean & Marie, whose farms laid the foundation of my deep connection and love of agriculture, nature, and land stewardship.

Every farm family I've had the privilege to serve — as an advisor, auctioneer, broker, or mediator — has, in their own way, honored the same legacy, values, and spirit of the family farm that I grew up on. For that, I am forever grateful. To my family and my clients, thank you for emboldening me with the passion to continue this work. To walk alongside others, to honor their histories, and to help the next generation of farmers and landowners honor and steward these precious resources.

May the work we do together continue to enrich lives for generations to come — and help our rural communities thrive, one farm at a time.

Acknowledgements

This book would not exist without the guidance of my mentor, Edward Geswein, who began serving farm families in 1977. Ed graciously welcomed me into his organization many years ago and allowed me to learn by his side through countless mediations, family farm negotiations, and thousands of acres of uniquely complex farmland transactions.

His philosophy of working with farm families and heirs with patience, empathy, and deep respect became a guidepost for me in my formative years. Those principles still shape how I show up for the families I serve today.

The foundation of my advisory and consulting work rests, in many ways, on the lessons Ed passed on to me. His impact continues to ripple outward in every conversation I have, every legacy I help preserve, and every family I'm privileged to serve.

Contents

A Handbook for Farm Heritage and Hope

As someone who has spent a lifetime deeply connected to the land — as a farmer, a policymaker, and an advocate for agricultural stewardship — I have come to recognize that our greatest assets are more than just fertile soil and productive acres. Our greatest assets are the values, experiences, and legacies cultivated through generations of family farmers and landowners.

Serving as Deputy Secretary of Agriculture at USDA provided me with the privilege of seeing American agriculture through a broader lens. Yet, my heart and my life's work remain rooted on my family farm in Indiana, where my wife and I have nurtured the land, watched our children grow, and where today, I practice regenerative agriculture. Our family's farm isn't merely a source of income — it is our home, our heritage, and our responsibility.

In *American Family Farmland*, Johnny Klemme uniquely captures the essence of what it truly means to inherit farmland today. This book isn't just about financial decisions or estate planning, although it covers these topics extensively. More importantly, it guides families through the emotional, relational, and legacy-driven complexities that inevitably surface when the future of a family farm is discussed.

The stories Johnny shares resonate deeply with me, echoing the challenges, opportunities, and values that I have encountered firsthand, both as a farmer and as someone entrusted with agricultural leadership at a national level. Whether your family is wrestling with questions about succession, stewardship, or financial strategy, this book serves as a wise companion, illuminating the paths forward and encouraging meaningful conversations around the kitchen table.

I encourage every farmer and landowner facing these critical crossroads to reflect carefully on the insights and practical wisdom offered within these pages. Johnny's empathetic and knowledgeable approach will help your family align decisions with core values, ensuring your land remains a source of pride, security, and fulfillment for generations to come.

As you turn these pages, may you find guidance, purpose, and a renewed commitment to stewarding not just your land but your family's most enduring legacy.

— **JIM MOSELEY,** *Farmer, Former Deputy Secretary of Agriculture, USDA*

This book serves as a wise companion, illuminating the paths forward and encouraging meaningful conversations around the kitchen table.

So, You've Inherited the Farm

Now what?

A farm is far more than just a piece of real estate; it is a teacher, imparting lessons about patience, perseverance, and the value of hard work. A classroom where dedication bears fruit season after season. It's a sanctuary for family gatherings, laughter-filled stories around the kitchen table, and wisdom passed down through generations. It's a living testament to family heritage, resilience, and deep-rooted connections to the land itself.

Yet, as we honor this rich legacy, inheriting the family farm can also mean navigating a maze of unexpected challenges and painful realities. Many farm families find that what begins as a cherished inheritance can quickly turn into a source of emotional strain and financial pressure. It can bring out tensions between siblings, highlight misunderstandings between farming and non-farming heirs, and even fracture relationships that once felt unbreakable.

If you're experiencing something like this, take heart — you're not alone. There is hope.

When making decisions about farmland, many families understandably start by focusing solely on financial returns, tax implications, or practical matters. While these are certainly important, they're only part of the bigger picture. Within these pages, you'll go beyond the financial ledger to put your family's values, emotional well-being, personal dreams, and relationships at the very heart of the decision-making process. Rather than simply making transactional choices, you'll be empowered to make thoughtful, intentional decisions that enrich your life, support your family, and align deeply with your vision of what truly matters.

Throughout my years advising farm families, I've discovered an important truth: No matter how overwhelming or emotionally charged your current circumstances feel, inheriting a family farm is ultimately a good challenge to face. Even if the situation carries deep feelings of grief, discord, or uncertainty, hidden within it are opportunities for more than just financial wealth. You'll discover opportunities for a deeper, richer form of wealth that includes personal growth, strengthened family bonds, shared values, and the creation of a meaningful, lasting legacy.

Within this book, you'll not only find philosophical insights and real-life family stories but also straightforward checklists, clear decision-making frameworks, and actionable strategies that you can start implementing immediately.

When a farm transitions from one generation to the next, it marks a meaningful milestone for everyone involved. And although you and your family members might not yet see eye to eye or even know exactly what to do next, I promise that with patience, clarity, and the right guidance, you will find a path forward that respects everyone's needs and goals.

The key is to adopt a mindset that allows you to view your farm as much more than a financial asset or piece of property. Instead, think of your inheritance as a unique opportunity to write your next chapter, pursue lifelong dreams, and create a lifestyle filled with purpose and joy. Perhaps you'll even discover ways to pass this priceless gift forward, endowing future generations with something meaningful and enduring.

This approach isn't merely about farm management or financial transactions; it's about defining and embracing a concept called Return on Life (ROL). While the phrase "Return on Life" is often used in the financial planning world, I've adapted this concept over the years to reflect something deeper for the farm families I work with. For me, Return on Life is a mindset — a lens for making decisions not just about money, but about meaning, well-being, and the life you want to live with your land, your family, and your future.

Importantly, a Return on Life mindset isn't a one-size-fits-all formula. It's deeply personal, requiring you to consider your individual goals, family dynamics, emotional values, and life aspirations. This perspective encourages thoughtful reflection, honest family dialogue, and professional consultation to navigate complexities and avoid unintended consequences.

By adopting a Return on Life approach to deciding what to do with inherited farmland, you'll be empowered to make informed, meaningful decisions that respect both the economic and emotional significance of your land. This ensures your decisions resonate beyond immediate financial outcomes, providing lasting value, no matter how you define it in your life.

Whether you intend to keep the farm in the family or you determine it's best to let it go at some point in the future, you are not alone in making this often once-in-a-lifetime decision. This book represents years of heartfelt conversations I've had while sharing meals at kitchen tables, exchanging thoughts on truck tailgates at sunset, walking thoughtfully through freshly planted fields, observing old fence lines and weathered wooden posts, and experiencing firsthand the powerful emotional connections farm families have with their land. I've seen how these connections to family traditions resonate deeply across generations.

Unfortunately, the story of the family farm sometimes includes scenes that are focused on disputes — siblings arguing over management roles, disagreements about selling or keeping the farm, or conflicts rooted in differing visions for the land. And these dramatic tales often overshadow the more positive, collaborative outcomes. But what if, instead of discord, your story became one of understanding, well-being, and a Return on Life that endures for generations?

In these pages, you'll find relatable, real-life stories from families who have faced situations much like yours. You'll gain practical steps and strategies that you can start using today to determine whether keeping your farm, selling it, or exploring creative versions of both scenarios is the best path toward achieving your personal and family goals. You'll encounter helpful checklists, actionable to-dos, and some tough, yet necessary questions that will encourage you and your family members to reflect deeply as you plan your farm's future. And you'll see how decisions guided by ROL principles can help you achieve far more than traditional measures of success by providing ways to ease tension, enhance communication, and strengthen relationships, offering a profound sense of reassurance that your choices align deeply with your family's shared values and individual dreams.

This book is your trusted companion — one that acknowledges the emotional weight of your decision, celebrates your family's history, and guides you toward outcomes that resonate profoundly with your own personal vision of success and fulfillment.

Above all, remember this: You have inherited an extraordinary opportunity to honor your past, clarify your present, and confidently create your future. Let's embark on this journey together, embracing the true value of your family farm in a way that reflects your goals, dreams, values, and the family ties you hold dear.

Additional Resources

You can find additional downloads, guides, and more practical steps to enriching the value of your land and life by visiting AmericanFamilyFarmland.com/downloads.

HEART, HERITAGE, AND HARD DECISIONS:

The True Value of Your Farm

CHAPTER 1

Farm Families 101: Every Acre Has a Story

"Be kind, for everyone you meet is fighting a hard battle."
— IAN MACLAREN

Pat was up late again, staring at papers and making notes long after everyone else had gone to bed. He wanted to be sleeping, too — after all, he had to get up for work tomorrow. But he had no choice in the matter.

It had only been a few months since his mother passed away, and Pat was named as the executor of his parents' will. As a result, he found himself the sole person tasked with the monumental task of deciding what to do next with their multi-generation family farm.

Making him executor was a logical decision. Pat was no stranger to farming. He'd spent his entire life in agriculture, working both on and off the land through his job at the local co-op. For decades, he farmed side by side with his dad, carrying the rhythms of planting, harvest, and all the decisions in between.

When his father passed, it was Pat who stepped in. He found a new tenant to work the land; someone he trusted to carry the torch forward. And even then, Pat hadn't fully stepped away. Each spring and fall, he returned to the farm to lend a hand with planting and harvest, staying connected not just to the work but to the place itself.

A few of Pat's siblings lived nearby, but most were scattered across the country, thousands of miles removed. On several occasions since his dad had passed away, one sibling or another would call him to say, "You know, Pat, we're going to have to figure out what to do with the farm at some point." But at the time, their concerns weren't an emergency. After all, their mom was still alive. Everything was going along all right.

Until now.

Every long, late night, Pat found himself reading over his parents' last will and testament and a stack of other estate planning documents, trying to figure out the complexities of the farm's inheritance stipulations. It felt like having a second job, and the stress was starting to take its toll.

His youngest daughter, Nancy, noticed his weariness one night during a dinner visit and said, "Dad, you look exhausted. Are you working too hard or what?"

"It's not work, it's the farm," he replied. "They all expect me to be the one who brings everyone together and finds the right answer. And I get it — this farm is important to all of us. It's our inheritance. I want to make sure we do the right thing for everyone. But carrying that kind of pressure alone? It's exhausting."

She listened, her eyes wide with concern as he went on. "You know I want to retire in five years, early enough that I can enjoy it. But as I get older, I know there's going to be medical bills, and your mom wants to add to the grandkids' college funds." He rubbed his temples, trying to make the headache starting there go away.

Earlier that summer, while the entire family was in town for their mother's funeral, they had gathered together at the farm. It was a celebration of life, a trip down memory lane, and also a time when some difficult conversations about the farm took place.

One by one, each of Pat's eight siblings took him aside to voice their concerns, their worries, and a lot of problems they had in their own lives. As executor, he needed to listen, but the conflicts weren't easy to manage. Some felt that the way their parents had divided up their assets just wasn't fair.

After one particularly tense exchange with his brothers, Pat watched in dismay as his younger brother, Bill, walked out, shaking his head and muttering that nobody was really listening. Pat felt the weight of the room shift and wished, not for the first time, that he wasn't stuck in the middle.

Bill's frustration wasn't just about the farm — it was about being heard. And Pat, overwhelmed and stretched thin, wasn't sure how to bridge the gap.

As the day wound down, Pat saw his eldest daughter, Kelly, rocking gently on the front porch swing of the old farmhouse. He sat down beside her and let out a big sigh. A long, deep breath followed. Kelly seemed to sense his weariness, and perhaps some of his uneasiness and frustration.

As he relished this moment of peace and quiet, Kelly gently grabbed his hand. "Dad, I think you need to talk to someone outside the family about all of this. I know just the right person."

A CALL FOR HELP

It was late spring. The crops were growing, and summer was quickly approaching, when I got a message from my childhood friend on Facebook.

"Can you give me a call?" the message read. "We need some advice about the farm."

"Sure," I replied.

I'd known Kelly nearly my entire life. We'd grown up in the same small town and had bonded throughout school, 4-H projects, and Indiana summer nights shared with friends.

I immediately picked up the phone and dialed Kelly's number. A few rings later, she picked up. "What's going on?" I asked, concerned.

Kelly's familiar voice was filled with her own concern. "Johnny, thanks for calling so quickly. My dad and his brothers and sisters just don't know what to do. Grandma passed away recently, and the farmer said he'd like to buy the land. They're not sure it's the right time to sell, and I am not even sure if they are all on the same page. Dad's the executor, so he's in the middle of all of this. Nancy said he's struggling to find a solution that keeps everyone happy and protects their inheritance. I've never seen him look so worn out. Would you mind sitting down with him over a cup of coffee for a conversation?"

That Saturday, I met with Pat and his wife, Jenny. We sat down at their kitchen table, and just as I took my first sip of coffee, Pat's phone rang.

Looking at the caller ID, he rolled his eyes. "Excuse me for just a minute, but I have to take this call; it's about the farm."

When he returned, he explained that the caller was his sister Janet, who lived in Texas. Janet's husband had been pressuring her to speak up about the farm, pressing for it to get it sold, and wondering why it was all taking so long. Janet was just as frustrated about the situation as her husband.

Seeing the weariness on Pat's face, I felt for him. Some of his family members were on the same page, but it was clear that the decision about what to do next was a difficult cross for him to bear, and he needed help. The more I learned about Pat and the pressure he felt as executor, the more I recognized how my own family farm experience was turning out to be a blessing in disguise. As we began to talk, we slowly put together some next steps for handling the situation with his family. The first was to get everyone in the same room.

Pat sighed heavily and shook his head, rubbing his tired eyes. "Johnny, I'll be honest with you. Getting everyone in the same room again is the last thing I want right now. Last time we tried that, it was a disaster." I listened in dismay as he told me about Bill's outburst at their mother's funeral.

Pat looked away, staring out the kitchen window at the fields stretching into the distance, then continued quietly, "I never wanted to be the referee. I didn't sign up to judge what's fair for each of my siblings, but somehow, here I am." His voice dropped lower, almost as if he were confessing something painful. "I keep thinking, *What would Dad have done? What would Mom want?* But they're not here to tell me anymore, and I feel like I'm letting them down every step of the way."

I nodded. "I'm sorry you're going through all of this," I said. "It sounds like a rough time for everyone, but especially you, being in the middle like this."

But I'd seen this before — strong, thoughtful people, carrying the emotional weight of decisions no one prepared them for. But I also knew they didn't have to carry the burden alone.

Pat nodded, swallowing. "Every choice I make feels wrong, like somebody loses no matter what. Janet's angry calls, Bill walking away upset — it wears on me. Sometimes, I just wish I could walk away too." He paused, looking directly at me now, earnest and searching for answers. "It's more than just money or land. This is about our family. If we get this wrong, what happens to us? That's what really keeps me up at night."

THE FAMILY MEETING

Though Pat dreaded another meeting, he agreed it was necessary. A month later, the entire family, spouses and all, gathered once again at the farm. This time, I was invited, too.

As I made my way down a scenic country road to meet Pat's family, I was calmly reminded of so many similarities to our own family farm. When I slowly pulled into the driveway, a large tabby cat scurried through a partially opened barn door. A string of rusty horseshoes hung from a nearby fuel tank, and I could see a broken-down tractor near the edge of an old shed, its hood missing and the paint faded by the sun.

I already knew we'd face some challenges during this evening's gathering. Pat told me he'd gotten another call earlier in the day from his brother Bill, who'd just landed at the airport and was driving to the farm for the big meeting.

"Pat, listen to what I am saying," Bill said. "What are we going to do about this farm? I get that our tenant wants to buy it, but if we sell it to him at that price, we'll barely have enough money to split between all of us. Hell, do we even know if the bank will lend him the money for it?"

"That's what we're going to talk about," Pat had replied. "Let's just talk when you get here." He wanted to get off the phone as quickly as possible. He didn't want any more stress before the meeting, which would be hard enough.

Pat was one of eight siblings, so I wasn't surprised when I saw a few people I didn't know standing in the yard as I parked my trusty pickup truck in the barn lot. One of them nodded and offered a halfhearted wave. The look he gave me felt polite, but a bit cold and aloof. He kept his distance as I approached, and I wondered if this was Bill, whom I'd already heard so much about. More likely, it was Roger, Pat's eldest sibling. Seven years older than Pat, he was, according to Pat, "a bit rough around the edges."

Pat was the first to greet me, and he started making introductions as we climbed a series of cracked concrete steps into a screened-in porch. The view of the farm was incredible, and it was clear that the memories made in that old farmhouse were tied to the farm like deep roots in the soil. I believe that when the land whispers, we must listen, and as I walked into the biggest room of their childhood home on the farm, I was reminded once again that while the land holds our past, it also has the power to shape our future.

That thought didn't make me feel any more reassured, though. As I looked out across the room, I felt like a deer in the headlights as 18 people sat facing me. Several folks sat on wooden kitchen chairs at the table, a few others sat themselves down on metal folding chairs, one person was perched on the edge of the counter, while others stood in the doorway of the kitchen, peeking around the corner, almost as if they wished they didn't have to be there.

I took a seat at the kitchen table, slowly opened my briefcase, and began to pass out a series of folders and documents; paperwork I'd spent hours preparing, refining, and perfecting for this one big meeting and moment. On my left sat the man who'd been a little aloof outside — and who I'd accurately guessed was Roger.

As I began to introduce myself, explain why I'd been invited, and how I would be able to help, I saw a fist raise high above the kitchen table out of the corner of my eye. It slammed down just a few inches from where I sat, and both the table and I practically jumped off the floor.

"Why the hell do we need your help anyway? We've already got an offer on the table," Roger exclaimed, his voice booming throughout the old farmhouse. His tone rang with aggression and frustration, and I knew this moment would stick with me for the rest of my career.

His point was made. The room went silent.

Looking back, I can see that his anger wasn't about me. It was about fear. About loss. About wanting something simple in a situation that was anything but.

The next several moments felt like an eternity, and I wouldn't have been surprised if the sound of my heart beating was heard by everyone in the room. Slowly and thoughtfully, I began shuffling and organizing all of the detailed reports, research, contracts, maps, charts, graphs, and market analysis that were part of my fully researched presentation and due diligence, laid out on the table in front of us.

As I began sliding the presentation back inside my briefcase, I said, "Before you say yes to the offer already on the table, just know that you don't have to hire us. In fact, you could put a 'For Sale' sign in the yard tomorrow, if that feels right."

Looking around the room, I said, "If you believe this offer is fair for everyone in this room, if you feel confident negotiating one of the largest transactions your family will ever make, if you've considered the tax implications, the legal mechanics, and how this sale will affect each person's future, then truly, there's no obligation. I'll respect that."

I watched as my words settled onto everyone in the room.

"My job," I added, "is to take a deep dive into the financial reality of your situation. To uncover the farm's true value. To weigh the hidden costs, the timing, and the tax angles, and to help you explore the best path forward so you don't leave tens or even hundreds of thousands of dollars on the table. And, as evidenced by all of you gathering here today, it seems that you're seeking a solution that feels right and makes everyone happy."

I looked around at their expressions. Some looked worried, others seemed skeptical, and others were unreadable.

"So?" I asked, gently. "Have you thought about how this might impact your retirement? Your Social Security? What about estate goals? Or how the proceeds will be divided? How will this affect your next generation? Will it be enough for peace of mind or for what's next?"

I wasn't pressing them. I was protecting them from making a rushed decision they might regret.

Then I closed the folder and said plainly, "If you're sure you can do this on your own, honestly, I understand. But if any part of this feels too big to carry alone, just know you don't have to."

I said it calmly. No pressure. No frustration. Just a clear invitation to reflect.

With a subtle shift in my chair, I moved to close my briefcase and thank everyone for their time.

A SHIFT IN EMOTION

At that exact moment, Pat also stood up and asked everyone to calm down, "Whoa! Now hold on just a minute, please. We're at a crossroads, and this is a life-changing decision. Some of us have traveled from thousands of miles away and gathered here because this decision affects us all."

Looking around at everyone, Pat continued. "We may not agree on the best way to handle Mom and Dad's farm, but that is just one of many reasons why I asked Johnny to be here. We need someone to help us understand the process, to listen to our concerns, and, more than anything, we need to lean on someone with professional experience so we do it right the first time. We only get one chance at this." He took a breath. "Now, I can only speak for myself and Jenny, but this decision could help us retire early. I know we all just want to come up with a solution so that we can all move forward."

With that, we all sat back down.

I pulled my presentation back out of my briefcase and slowly began walking the family through what needed to happen next. I explained the overall process, expectations, timelines, and communication. I outlined the strategies we'd use and highlighted how we'd always be mindful of the unique goals and needs of every person around the table.

As the discussion deepened, Pat's brother Bill leaned forward, his voice tense. "I don't even want to sell the farm. This is our parents' legacy, and we're just going to toss it away... for the money?"

Without missing a beat, Roger replied, "Are you going to come up with a few million dollars to keep it?" Once again, the entire room went silent. Bill said nothing, his expression heavy, his shoulders lowered.

After an hour or so of discussion, we hadn't yet discovered a clear path forward.

Still, we kept going.

Another hour or so — and several breaks to cool heads and clear minds — and the questions gave way to deeper understanding. The tension began to shift.

We covered everything from title work to deeds, disclosures, and chain of title. But we also talked about what really mattered: the people. The past. The story behind the land. As we discussed the farm's legacy, the hard work their parents and grandparents had poured into this land, and how we could honor the spirit of the farm, Roger once again stood up.

He looked slowly around the room, making deliberate eye contact with every sibling and in-law. Then he clasped his hands in front of him and closed his eyes for just a moment, as if steadying himself.

When he spoke, his voice was quiet, but clear.

"Mom and Dad gave us a gift. This, right now, is our moment of truth. And if what I've heard from each of you tonight is true, then my vote is to put our faith in this plan we've seen here tonight. Let's let Johnny and his team get to work."

There were murmurs of agreement, and as I looked around the room, I saw tears and hesitancy, but I also saw relief. I suddenly realized that Roger's initial harsh exclamation had been sadness disguised as anger. He was still mourning the loss of his parents and was frustrated that all of the heirs were not on the same page.

That night, as Pat's family filed out of the farmhouse, the mood felt changed. They didn't have any final answers yet, but there was something different about their attitudes now. There was a willingness to keep talking. A shared sense of direction. Pat had their agreement that they would talk it over as a family, and we'd meet again soon.

As Pat and I walked to our trucks, he looked directly at me. His eyes welled up and he said to me, "Listen, Johnny, I really don't want our family to sell the farm, but I don't have a couple million dollars lying around and I just can't buy my family members out. If there were some way to keep part of it, or a way for the spirit of the family farm to continue, and there is enough money to go around, that really would probably be the best win-win for everyone."

I nodded once. "Let's see what we can do."

TOP CONCERNS OF FARM INHERITORS

Pat's situation wasn't unusual. If anything, it highlighted just how layered and emotional farm inheritance decisions can be. His story might seem complex, but I share it to show what's possible. With the right perspective and the right help, families like yours can find a clear way forward. If Pat and his siblings could navigate their thorny set of problems, you can too. You just need some guidance on what factors to consider and how to go about finding the answers you need.

Over the years, I've worked alongside hundreds of farmers, families, heirs, trustees, executors, and their advisors, including attorneys, accountants, wealth managers, and others. There are a significant number of challenges and issues that come with inheriting a farm. It's a financial decision. It's an emotional decision. It's a family decision. And it's a legacy decision. What I've learned is that no two farms are alike. Each family brings its own set of priorities, pressures, and history to the table, which is something I love about my work.

Across the hundreds of thousands of acres of farmland transactions and a significant number of farm management decisions, I've found that some concerns come up time and again — questions that families ask when faced with the weight of inherited land. Here are the top concerns I run into the most often, in one way or another:

1. **Should we keep it, sell it, or lease it?** This is often the first — and hardest — question families face. The answer depends on your values, financial goals, emotional attachments, and practical realities. Each path has its own challenges and opportunities.

2. **What's the farm's worth?** Understanding market value, soil quality, income potential, and appraisal options is essential for making informed decisions. Some families overestimate their farm's value based on emotional attachment, while others underestimate the value of the land they're holding. Depending on the local market, values may even be lower than expectations. Realistic expectations are critical.

3. **How will taxes impact us?** Estate tax, capital gains tax, income tax, and property taxes all come into play. Many families aren't sure what tools are available and how things like 1031 exchanges, charitable trusts, and installment sales might help. That's where good advisors make all the difference.

4. **What if there's more than one heir?** Undivided interest (tenants-in-common) or joint tenancy can make decision-making difficult. Conflict often arises when family members want different things, or the expectation of inheritance differs from the realities, especially when a person is emotionally or financially tied to the land. Mediation and facilitation can prevent long-term conflict, tension, or resentment.

5. **What about existing tenants?** If the farm is leased, existing agreements matter. Tenants have rights. Contracts have terms. And changes should be made with care. Families often feel stuck between loyalty and legal obligation, especially when a tenant is also a relative. Breaking a lease early or rushing toward a sale without taking the lease into consideration could have consequences.

6. **What if one of my family members is the farmer?** Family dynamics can get complicated. This could add another layer of challenges to the decision-making process. Fairness and coming to an agreement without conflict can be challenging. Fortunately, an experienced advisor can guide you through the process of making the right decision for everyone.

7. **How do we manage the farm if we're not farmers?** Many heirs have strong professional skills, but farming

isn't one of them. That's okay. A great farm manager or advisor can help you care for the land wisely, without needing to be in the field yourself.

8. **Can we afford to keep the farm?** Maintenance. Taxes. Equipment. Insurance. Repairs. They add up. Many families underestimate what it really costs to own farmland, especially when they're not generating enough revenue to cover those expenses.

9. **Is now the right time to sell?** Some families feel an urgency to sell quickly. Others want to hold out for a stronger market. Timing matters, and so does understanding the local landscape, buyer trends, and comparable sales. Smart decisions start with good data, not rushed decisions.

10. **Are there conservation or stewardship considerations?** Many families want to do right by the land. Some farms have easements or conservation considerations that require special attention. Others want to explore long-term ways to preserve open space, wildlife habitat, woods or timber stands, and water quality.

11. **Are we legally prepared?** The inheritance process isn't always smooth. Wills. Trusts. Deeds. Probate. Title issues. Affidavits. Missing paperwork. Conflicting heirs. These are more common than you might think, and they can stall or derail progress if not addressed early.

12. **How do we handle the emotional weight?** Even when selling makes financial sense, the emotional struggle can be overwhelming. Farms often hold memories,

identity, and a sense of purpose. Moving forward means giving yourself permission to grieve and grow at the same time.

13. **How do we stay profitable with rising costs?** For families still operating the farm, the financial head-winds are real and include higher costs for inputs, labor, fuel, and equipment. Having a strategic, resilient plan and a clear understanding of cash flow is more essential than ever.

14. **How do we find and keep good help?** Whether you're hiring full-time labor or relying on seasonal support, finding reliable, skilled farmhands is getting harder. Workforce challenges often shape a family's long-term decision about whether to keep the farm at all.

COMPLICATING ELEMENTS

The problems farm inheritors have to address get tougher when multiple heirs have differing opinions about what to do. The same complexity can occur when there's only one heir with internal conflicts pulling them in multiple directions. In these situations, heirs often get stuck and feel like there's no good way forward. Conflicts and disagreements bubble to the surface, further complicating the situation. Everyone gets frustrated, and they want to be finished with the whole decision-making process.

This leads to maybe the most important question of all: Can we make a decision that respects everyone, and still feels right?

Yes, you can.

And you don't have to do it alone.

LET'S START GETTING SOME ANSWERS

The first problem most families have when they find themselves in this situation is believing the answers to all their questions start with a spreadsheet. They think they have to figure out the numbers and logistics, but that's why they get stuck. In reality, the numbers won't give you what you need until you get some more important answers that look at deeper values and motivations. Those answers start with you.

Start by asking yourself these questions:

- What matters most to me right now?
- Why does it matter?
- What do I truly want for my family, my finances, and my peace of mind?

Why do the answers to these questions matter? You'll find out as you work your way through the chapters of this book.

And what if you don't know how to answer those questions yet? That's okay. You will.

By reading this book, you're already on your way. I'm about to take you through the same process I took Pat and his family through. It worked for them and every one of my clients, and it can work for you, too.

And in case you're wondering how I know how this feels, it's simple: I've been through this same experience myself.

CHAPTER 2

Tough Decisions: When My Family Sold Our Farm

"I just don't see how there's any other choice."

I heard my father's words as I stepped into my parents' house, my boots still covered with dust from the barn. The familiar sound of the wind chimes outside carried through the open kitchen window, their tune blending with the low murmur of conversation.

Dad sat at the kitchen table, elbows resting heavily on the worn wooden surface, his head in his hands. My mother, sitting beside him, reached across to gently squeeze his forearm. "I'm sorry, dear," she whispered.

That's when I knew.

They were talking about selling the farm.

I'd known this moment might come. Everyone's mood had shifted after my grandfather passed away earlier in the year, and I could feel the undercurrent pulling us toward the difficult decisions looming ahead. But still, I'd held onto the hope that those decisions were far off — that they belonged to another lifetime.

Like so many farm families, Dad had siblings, each with their own needs, goals, and expectations. Grandma was now on her own in an assisted living facility, and the pressure to sell the farm was building. And while every member of the family had their own deep-rooted ties to the land, it was Mom and Dad who'd spent their life working the soil, rising with the sun, putting their faith in the seeds planted, and tending to the acres that had been our livelihood.

> I'd held onto the hope that those decisions were far off — that they belonged to another lifetime.

But now, selling the farm was inevitable.

Even though we'd seen it coming, saying it aloud still felt like letting go of something sacred.

The next morning, I walked the farm, trying to press each memory into my mind so I could hold on to every sight, every scent, every sound.

Along a fencerow, I ran my hands across the rough edge of an old cattle gate, its chain still wrapped tightly around a worn wooden post. I remembered the winter morning when we hammered a nail into that post after our small herd of cattle had broken out of the pasture, only to be found hours later wandering through the local cemetery. I'd felt a bit of an adrenaline rush as we herded them home on horseback. For a brief moment, it seemed as though we were real cowboys.

I passed a small wooden shed, peered through the dusty glass of an old window, and saw a leather bridle still hanging on a horseshoe. It had belonged to Bandit, a horse with a Texas brand and a mischievous streak. He knew he didn't have to work unless you could get a rope over his neck, so he'd prance just out of reach, kicking up dust, testing my patience as a young cowboy. But once I caught him, he'd let me saddle him up, and we'd ride off into the sunset like old friends.

In the same shed, a faded blue ribbon hung over the edge of a dusty shelf — one of many from ten years of 4-H competitions, county fairs, and early mornings spent tending to horses, cattle, pigs, and rabbits. Each year brought new lessons, not just about farming, but about responsibility, discipline, and perseverance. Everywhere I turned, I saw bits of my childhood frozen in time.

Every corner of the farm held a story. And with every memory, I felt the land tugging at me — not just to remember it, but to mourn what we were about to lose.

Walking past the tool shed, I noticed the metal door swaying in the wind, clanking softly against the wall. An old barn cat slinked through the opening, focused, and on the hunt for a field mouse nearby.

Inside the shop, the basketball hoop still hung above the weathered concrete floor. A half-flattened leather ball lay in the corner; a quiet reminder of pickup games played after long days in the field and with cousins at every family gathering.

I climbed an old, rusty auger outside the corn crib and peered into the loft — a place that was once the perfect hide-and-seek spot. The space was half-filled with forgotten straw bales and likely, a few raccoons. It had been years since I'd ventured up there, but the sense of adventure still clung to the air.

At the western edge of the property sat two silver grain bins. Their fans still; their purpose fulfilled. Climbing to the top of one, I let out a big sigh.

As kids, we used to sit up here, watching the sky change from gold to deep purple, fireflies flickering in the fields below. The golden-hour light danced across weathered barns and grain bins, turning them into silhouettes etched against the sky. A gentle breeze carried the earthy scent of freshly tilled soil. Back then, the sunsets felt like a closing chapter of the day. But today, as the sky darkened, it felt like the end of an era.

I took a deep breath, and with another big exhale, I could feel a tear begin to well up and roll down my cheek. With each passing moment, the sun dipped further below the horizon.

I made my way back to the house, and as I stepped back inside, I pulled off my boots on the first step of the garage just like I'd done since I was old enough to work alongside my dad and grandfather. The house still smelled like faint traces of coffee, home-cooked meals, and time itself. A cabinet door stood slightly ajar, revealing a dust-covered CB radio. The excitement from my childhood came rushing back at the sight.

"Breaker one-nine, this is Pine Tree Base. Do you copy, Dad?"

That's what I'd say every afternoon when I got home from school, my fingers wrapped around the heavy microphone, its curly cord stretched to its limit.

The moment he answered was magic.

"Hello, Pine Tree Base. How ya doing, little buddy?"

If he was close, I'd race through the field to meet him and climb into the cab of the tractor to ride along until dark. If he was miles away, I'd wait anxiously for Mom to pack up orange and yellow Tupperware containers, sun-soaked iced tea, bread and butter, and homemade meatloaf and mashed potatoes in her favorite glass dishes — a field meal, delivered with love.

The ground where my boots once kicked up dust, where we stacked rocks along the fencerows, where we shared meals and built a livelihood? Those acres are no longer ours. But the farm, in many ways, still lives on. Now, it exists in the photographs that hang on the walls of my family's homes.

A black-and-white image of my grandfather standing in a pasture full of turkeys, his face just starting to weather from years in the field. A picture of my father in front of the deep green soybean fields I ran through as a child, the sun setting behind him. A framed snapshot of my dad and his siblings, their jeans stained with dirt, with the family dog, two old tractors, and Grandpa grinning after a long day in the field.

Our family's farm may be gone, but the photographs tell its story. They're proof that the land shaped us, that the values we learned there endure, and that the legacy of our farm will always have a home in our hearts.

A NEW PURPOSE

Years later, after saving, planning, and dreaming, I bought my own 30-acre farm just one county away from where our old family farm once stood.

One evening, I sat in a rocking chair on the porch watching fireflies flicker across different fields under the same kind of Indiana sky I'd grown up beneath. A gentle breeze whispered through the oak tree nearby, its leaves rustling in rhythm with the frogs, crickets, and the low song of a mourning dove in the distance.

It was peaceful. Beautiful. Familiar. And something inside me stirred.

Looking at this perfect scene on my own farm reminded me of all the moments, memories, and cherished times from my childhood. That evening, with the quiet all around, it hit me: The pain of losing our farm hadn't disappeared. But over time, it had turned into a calling. I couldn't undo what had happened, but I could use my experience to help others.

The decision my family had made to sell our farm out of necessity, pressure, and love was more than a transaction. It was the unraveling of something we believed would last forever.

And it was at that moment that I also realized the loss of my family's farm had given me my life's purpose. It came in pieces — conversations, quiet realizations, and the steady conviction that no one should have to navigate this alone.

Our family was fortunate to have outside support throughout the experience, but I knew not everyone was so lucky. I wanted to help families navigate the tough decision to keep or sell their farmland.

I couldn't undo what had happened to our farm, but I could help others. I could become the person who understood the emotional weight, the complexity, the nuances, the family dynamics, and the hard financial questions that come with inheriting a farm.

I could listen.

I could guide.

I could help families make decisions they wouldn't regret.

A CALLING ROOTED IN EXPERIENCE

The first person I turned to was Ed Geswein.

Ed had been a steady hand through my family's transition, advising my parents and their siblings during the sale of our farm and offering insight during a time when we were struggling to see clearly. More than that, he was a friend. A mentor. A quiet expert in some of the most emotional conversations farm families ever face.

He'd been consulting with landowners since 1977, and he understood something most people don't: that every acre carries more than market value. It carries identity, pressure, expectation, and family stories. He'd guided countless families, heirs, executors, and trustees, and worked hand in hand with their attorneys, wealth advisors, and CPAs through thousands of acres of transitions. And after every sale, he remained a friend and trusted advisor.

"I want to work with you," I told him. "I want to learn what you know."

The first time I sat in on a meeting with Ed and a farm family, I watched him listen — not just to what they said, but to what they didn't say. He had a way of asking questions that helped people see more clearly. He didn't try to "fix" their problems. He helped them find their own way through.

Over the years, Ed taught me what to look for in the tension in a room, a person's body language, the silence between words. He taught me about the numbers and hard data too. I saw how much it mattered to our clients to have someone who understood both the financial and emotional landscape of their situation.

Learning from Ed cemented the belief I'd felt in my heart that summer night on my front porch: Guiding families through the decision to keep or sell their farm was more than just something I wanted to do; it was the work I was meant to do.

Since then, I've sat at countless kitchen tables. I've ridden in combines beside farmers, met in the parking lots of rural churches, and walked fields with families who were trying to make the hardest decision of their lives.

Sometimes they're grieving. Sometimes they're overwhelmed. Sometimes they're just trying to hold their family together while figuring out what comes next.

In every conversation, my job is the same: To listen. To guide. And to help them move from confusion to clarity.

Eventually, I became a business partner with Ed and Craig Stevenson, another respected ag professional. And together, we've built something we're proud of: Geswein Farm & Land, a farm and land brokerage and consulting firm with offices in both Lafayette, Indiana, and Tuscola, Illinois. Our team has been recognized as one of America's Best Brokerages by the Land Report, and we've consistently been named among the Top Agricultural Real Estate Services Providers and Top Auction Companies in the country.

With the help of a dedicated team of certified appraisers, brokers, auctioneers, farm managers, and a trusted network of financial professionals, we've walked families through the succession, sale, or transition of thousands upon thousands of acres, guiding decisions that reflect not just financial outcomes, but family values, goals, and emotional peace.

We've earned national recognition for our work, but the moments we're proudest of happen at kitchen tables, in pickup trucks, and around family farm fields, helping people like you find peace and confidence in a difficult season. It's in the moments we've helped protect legacies while creating freedom.

That's why I love to tell farm stories. My documentary, *LAND VALUES*, was selected for the Smithsonian's *Water/Ways* exhibition and has been screened internationally. Our ongoing docuseries, *Stories of Stewardship*, continues to lift up the voices of farmers and families who are adapting, persevering, and leading in their communities.

I do this because the story of American farmland isn't ending. It's evolving. And I believe it's a story that deserves to be told with honesty, hope, and heart.

WHAT I WANT FOR YOU

Today, my family's farm has grown to 91 acres, and we're trying to live what we teach. We work to balance agriculture, conservation, and a vision for what legacy might look like one generation from now. We plant values of hard work, character, and leadership in the soil, in the forest, along the creek bank, and in our next generation so that whatever they build in the future, it's rooted in something meaningful that will lead to more than material and financial success, but toward their own well-being and higher purpose.

My work focuses on those same values and philosophies, and I've been fortunate to have helped families through hundreds of millions in farmland transactions in 2024 alone — a total that includes more than 12,000 acres passed from one generation to the next, 77,000 acres appraised and evaluated, and $56 million in auctions conducted across the Midwest.

We've walked with families as they've found answers. We've helped turn once-painful decisions into powerful turning points. And we've done it all with the belief that American farmland and the families stewarding the land deserve more than "business as usual."

That's what I want for the families I serve, including those I help through this book.

No two farms or families are the same. Every farm family needs to define what success looks like for *them*.

It might be preserving the farm for another generation. It might be selling with peace of mind. It might be finding a way to honor the past while building something new. Whatever it is, we begin with the end in mind.

Along the way, you deserve clarity. You deserve compassion. You deserve someone who will help you carry the weight of your decision without telling you what to do.

That's the work I'm passionate about, and that's what this book is here to help you do.

Though it can't give you all the answers, this book can help you find *your* answer.

Because your story, your values, and your future matter, and I'm honored to walk alongside you.

ARE YOU READY TO MOVE FORWARD?

This book will help you ask better questions, recognize what matters most, and take meaningful steps forward at your own pace, on your own terms. The answers you need aren't in someone else's blueprint — they're in the values, memories, and future you're trying to protect.

In the chapters that follow, we'll walk through real examples of families just like yours who found ways to navigate the emotional, financial, and relational weight of farmland decisions. You'll see the patterns, the possibilities, and the powerful outcomes that can happen when people stop avoiding the conversation and start leading with courage.

Deciding whether to keep or sell your inherited farm is about life. It's about you. It's about making a decision you can live with, and live *into*, for years to come.

So, take a deep breath. You've come this far.

Let's take the next step together.

CHAPTER 3

Looking Deeper: Understanding Your Values

One of the most common questions families ask me — often with quiet hesitation — is, "Are we doing the right thing if we sell the farm? If we keep it, what will it cost us?"

These aren't just financial questions. They're values questions. And the answers start by understanding what the farm truly means to each person around your table.

Your farm represents your grandparents' sacrifices and your family's memories. But alongside these cherished moments, there's also real tension, practical challenges, and difficult realities demanding thoughtful answers when you're faced with the decision to keep or sell your land.

In this chapter, we'll explore conflicting values carefully and honestly. We'll dive into why they happen, what they're really about, and most importantly, how you can begin finding common ground with your family so you can avoid getting stuck in an endless cycle of wondering what to do next.

Once you clearly understand the motivations beneath everyone's viewpoints, you'll start seeing real opportunities for solutions that balance emotion and practicality.

THE THREE TYPES OF VALUE

If you've ever found yourself sitting around the kitchen table wondering, "Why can't we just agree on what to do with the farm?" — you're not alone.

That tension often comes from something deeper than disagreement. It comes from each person valuing the farm in a different way and speaking a different emotional or practical language.

When family members talk about value, each person is often using language that represents their personal desires and motivations. Fortunately, Oxford Languages provides a helpful starting point, offering three distinct definitions of the word *value:*[1]

1. The importance, worth, or usefulness of something.
2. A person's principles or standards of behavior; one's judgment of what is important in life.
3. Estimate of monetary worth (of something).

Essentially, each person sitting around the table could be considering the emotional value, principle-based value, or financial value of the farmland.

For some family members, the farm is deeply tied to identity and memory. This is emotional value. It's the birthday parties in the old farmhouse, the sweet scent of freshly cut hay, or the

---

1   *Oxford English Dictionary*, 2025. https://www.oed.com/

comforting sound of the screen door closing on summer evenings. The thought of letting go feels like losing part of your family's story, a piece of your own identity. That emotional connection can be incredibly powerful and hard to put into words because it's hard to measure quantitatively. Instead, it's felt deeply, remembered vividly, and protected passionately.

For others, the farm is seen through a lens of duty or principle. Maybe you or another family member feels a strong responsibility to preserve what your parents or grandparents sacrificed to create. There's often a quiet but firm belief that honoring those who came before and those who will come after means protecting the land, no matter what. It's a deeply moral stance, rooted in a strong sense of what's right and meaningful. It's the voice that says, "We owe it to the generations before and after us to protect this place."

Then, there's the practical perspective that's impossible to ignore. Perhaps you're the one who clearly recognizes the financial realities like market values, managing debt, cash flow, retirement concerns, or the opportunities that selling, diversifying, or leasing could offer. Approaching the farm through this practical lens doesn't mean your emotional ties are weaker; it means you're looking realistically at your responsibilities and future possibilities.

It's important to remember that these different ways of seeing value aren't mutually exclusive. You might be actively farming, deeply attached to the land, but quietly aware of the financial pressures. Or perhaps your entire family is privately wrestling with an emotional attachment that feels at odds with practical realities you can't overlook.

That internal tension or subtle family conflict you're feeling is completely natural. It doesn't mean something's broken. It simply means there are deeply held, differing perspectives at play.

Identifying these value perspectives doesn't solve the tension, but it does help explain it. Once each person feels seen and heard, families can shift from defending positions to uncovering shared purpose.

The value chart that follows isn't a formula; it's a lens. Use it to ask better questions, not to "fix" each other's thinking.

Type of Value	What It Really Means	Common Expressions
Emotional	Family memories, identity, personal attachment	"This farm is our family's story; letting go feels impossible."
Principle-Based	Duty, moral beliefs, legacy preservation	"We have a responsibility to honor what past generations built."
Financial	Practical realities, measurable worth, market conditions	"We must be realistic and smart about what the land can do for us."

Understanding the different types of value helps everyone involved in the decision-making process see what's *beneath* the surface. And it can also reveal something else: opportunity.

Instead of arguing over dollars, families start talking about dreams and goals. They stop defending positions and start sharing their deeper desires. They go from thinking disagreements are failures to seeing conflicts as a starting point for creativity, compromise, and shared purpose. Your farm's greatest assets extend far beyond the fertile soil, woods, pastures, creeks, or equipment; they're found in the minds, hearts, goals, dreams, and ambitions of everyone around your table.

The key to moving forward is naming and understanding each perspective around your table, including your own. In Chapter 4, you'll learn how to pair your new understanding of your values with a Return on Life mindset and the LAND VALUES framework so you can clearly determine whether keeping or selling your inherited farmland is the best choice for you and your family.

> Your farm's greatest assets extend far beyond the fertile soil, woods, pastures, creeks, or equipment; they're found in the minds, hearts, goals, dreams, and ambitions of everyone around your table.

WHEN VALUES CREATE CONFLICT

Now that you've seen how value is defined differently by each person, let's look at what happens when those definitions collide in real families like Pat's.

You might recall the quiet tension Pat felt while trying to do right by every member of his family. Each conversation seemed to uncover new layers of complexity and new perspectives he hadn't fully anticipated. On top of each sibling's definition of value and desires for the farm was the gentle yet persistent weight of the memory of the decades of work and sacrifice his parents and grandparents had poured into the land.

Perhaps you can relate.

When farmland transitions between generations, it rarely comes with a roadmap or clear instructions. It certainly doesn't come with a single, universally agreed-upon definition of what the farm's real *value* is.

Instead, it brings pressure, expectations, assumptions, and family members each carrying their unique vision for what the farm should represent or become.

Sometimes these conflicts are subtle — an unspoken unease that fills quiet moments. Other times, they're loud and emotional, full of heated conversations that never seem to reach a resolution. And sometimes, even if you're the only heir to the land, the conflict may live entirely within you like a tug-of-war between your emotional ties and practical realities.

If any of this feels familiar, you're in the right place.

Let's look back at Pat's family for a moment. Roger, Pat, Bill, Janet, Mike, Linda, Dan, Sarah, and Josh each had a view of the farm that was shaped by personal needs, unspoken fears, past experiences, and very different definitions of what mattered most. So, before we talked about numbers, timelines, or strategy, we mapped out each family member's priorities.

The Frustrated Oldest Brother

Roger was loud. Angry. And adamant.

He didn't want to just "cash out," but he didn't want to drag things out either. He'd reached his breaking point when he shouted and slammed his fist on the table during our first meeting. Roger wasn't just angry about the delay; he was angry about the loss. Their parents were gone. Their family rhythm had shifted. And now, the farm — their anchor — was up for grabs.

His rage wasn't about the land. It was about not knowing what to hold onto next.

The Heartbroken

Bill didn't want to sell. But when asked if he could buy out the rest of the family, he fell silent.

He loved the land, but love doesn't always have millions in the bank. He was stuck between sentiment and practicality, and at the end of the day, he was unsure how to speak that truth without disappointing someone.

The Tired Out-of-Stater

Janet didn't feel deeply tied to the land, but she felt tied to the tension. Her phone calls were getting shorter, her tone more strained.

"Why is this taking so long?" she asked Pat over the phone. "This is dragging out way longer than it should. We just need to sell."

Janet's voice was tired, tinged with guilt and frustration. "Pat, you know it's not that I don't care about the farm. But Mark's business is in trouble. Sales are down, the loans keep piling up, and honestly, things are getting tight around here."

For Janet, it wasn't just her voice that mattered. She was speaking for her household. Her stress was the result of her fear of being seen as the "bad guy" in a decision she didn't want to make.

The Reluctant Decision-Maker

Pat didn't want to sell the farm either. But he also wasn't sure he wanted to buy the farm, or manage it, or carry it. He was five years away from retirement. He wanted time with his grandkids. He wanted peace. And while the money from a sale would help, it didn't feel like a win.

HELPING EVERYONE FEEL SEEN
AND UNDERSTOOD

Each sibling was carrying pressure, pain, memories, or hopes they hadn't said out loud. My job wasn't to label them — it was to help them feel seen.

If asked, Pat and his siblings probably would have said they shared the same values. They just didn't express them the same way. In addition, they were each in different situations, and they needed different things in their lives. As a result, they couldn't find common ground in making the decisions.

You've likely started reflecting on how the different definitions of value relate to your family's land, and perhaps you've begun noticing some tension within yourself or among family members. If so, take a moment to reflect honestly on the following questions. You don't need immediate answers, just clarity.

- Am I leaning most strongly toward emotional, principle-based, or financial value?
- Are others in my family viewing the farm from a different perspective?
- Have we clearly discussed these differences, or are we quietly making assumptions?

Maybe you're the person who spent a lifetime farming and feel every emotional attachment deeply while simultaneously managing daily practical realities. Or perhaps you're the sole heir, quietly vacillating between what your heart genuinely desires and what your logical mind knows you need to consider. Clearly naming these differences won't immediately solve everything, but it will create understanding. And understanding is the cornerstone for moving forward constructively.

As an advisor, my role is to step into these sensitive situations and gently help families articulate their values, hear each other more deeply, and find common ground. I help them uncover the deeper truths beneath surface-level disagreements. In these pivotal moments, families need conversations that honor everyone's perspective. It's important that the actively farming family member's wisdom and emotional connection are heard and valued alongside the practical insights of those who see the farm from different vantage points.

When every person — and, in fact, every *perspective* — is honored, the pressure to make the "perfect" decision eases. Instead of feeling paralyzed by fear or guilt, the decision makers start feeling empowered by possibility and clarity.

ALIGNING YOUR VALUES WITH YOUR GOALS

Before your family can align along a path forward, it helps to zoom out and ask, "What are we really hoping this land can do for us?"

This next section isn't about getting the right answer — it's about helping each person name what matters most to them in this season of life. These goals aren't obligations. They're possibilities.

Like Pat, you may understand how quickly the simple question "What should we do?" can escalate into frustration and disagreement. As you gather with your family and define what your values are, it can be helpful to think big picture by considering everyone's goals. First, consider the five categories of goals:

1. **Family and relationship.** This involves thoughtfully balancing inheritance decisions in a way that focuses not just on fairness, but on what truly supports the future. It can include preserving family unity, supporting aging parents or caregivers, leaving meaningful legacies to your children, resolving lingering conflicts, establishing new family traditions, and easing the burdens faced by the next generation.

2. **Lifestyle and well-being.** This includes achieving better work-life balance, reducing stress and mental fatigue, creating time and space for travel or personal growth, shaping a healthier environment for your family, pursuing education or skill-building, and improving quality of life for your spouse, children, or aging parents.

3. **Legacy and meaningful impact.** This includes honoring the work of previous generations, supporting environmental sustainability or conservation, preventing unwanted development, establishing philanthropic or community contributions, and preserving your family's story and heritage.

4. **Opportunity-based goals.** This includes exploring new careers or passions, relocating or acquiring different property, creating new income streams, enabling early retirement, and funding educational or creative dreams.

5. **Market timing and economic factors.** This includes selling at a strong market value, maximizing value through strategic planning, avoiding a potential dip or downturn, taking advantage of favorable tax conditions, responding to strong buyer interest, and calculating the opportunity cost of holding vs. selling.

To jump-start this goal-assessment process, I recommend asking everyone these three questions:

1. What role do you want the farm to play in your life?

This is one of the most important questions I ask families. And it often changes the conversation entirely because the truth is that not everyone sees the farm the same way. And not everyone *should*.

For some, the farm is financial security. It's a tangible, appreciating asset that generates income, provides a full-time livelihood, and helps preserve wealth. For others, it's a living memory of childhood, family traditions, and generations of hard work. For a few, it's a weekend retreat. A future homeplace. A retirement property. And for others still, it's something they want to protect, preserve, restore, or use for conservation and community.

Knowing where you stand is the foundation of clarity.

2. Is keeping the farm a smart wealth decision?

Once the emotional layers are named, it's time to look at the financial picture. Farmland is one of the most stable, inflation-resistant assets in any investment portfolio. According to USDA and private land data, farmland has appreciated at an average rate of 12.75% annually (including land appreciation and cash rent) over the long term, often outperforming more volatile assets like stocks and bonds. In other words, keeping the farm can be a *very* smart wealth move as long as it aligns with your broader financial goals.

Keeping the land requires thoughtful management, planning, and a long-term mindset. If you're keeping the farm purely out of sentiment and it's draining your resources or preventing other important financial moves, it may not be the best option for you. But if the land fits into your long-term financial strategy, or is your primary source of income, farmland can offer significant advantages and portfolio diversification that few other assets can match.

If keeping the farm aligns with your financial goals, then there are many tax advantages available to maximize your wealth over time. We'll take a closer look at those benefits in the next chapter as we explore the LAND VALUES framework.

3. Does keeping the farm fit your personal goals?

Does keeping the farm bring you peace? Does it give your family a way to stay connected, or is it a source of stress and obligation? Does keeping this farm support the kind of life you want to live and the kind of life you want for the people you love?

The answers to these questions will tell you more than any appraisal ever could.

The more clarity you build now, the easier it will be to make decisions that you feel good about later, so consider these five goal categories when you're deciding whether keeping or selling the farm aligns with your goals best.

FINDING YOUR FAMILY'S BEST PATH FORWARD

Families who successfully handle these tough choices don't rely on quick fixes or impulsive reactions. Instead, they adopt a thoughtful, practical strategy, and:

- **Slow down.** Quick decisions made under emotional pressure rarely turn out well. Give yourself space to reflect clearly, weigh your options, and avoid rushed choices you'll regret later.

- **Look at the big picture.** Step back and think through how each decision will affect you and your family, not just today, but years from now. Clearly evaluate the emotional, financial, and practical implications for everyone involved.

- **Truly listen.** Families reach their best outcomes when everyone's perspective is genuinely heard, even if it's challenging. Clearly understanding each other's values and priorities can reveal solutions everyone can embrace.

Whether you choose to keep the farm, lease it, restructure ownership, or thoughtfully sell, you need to feel you're moving forward with clarity, compassion, and confidence. The best decisions are always those that honor both the heart and the mind, respect the contributions of every family member, and reflect your family's unique story.

The families who experience the most success when faced with the decision to keep or sell their farm have one important thing in common: At a crucial moment — just like the one you may find yourself in right now — they pause and ask themselves:

- "What legacy do we truly want to leave behind?"
- "How can our choices empower the goals or dreams of each family member?"
- "How do we ensure our decisions respect and reflect everyone's unique contributions, ambitions, and emotional ties to the land?"

It's important to not only answer these questions honestly but also to choose to answer them as a team, making clear, meaningful choices everyone can feel genuinely proud of.

However, clarity doesn't always erase complexity. Often, as you begin exploring your deeper motivations and values, you'll uncover differences you didn't even realize were there. Rather than being obstacles to avoid, these conflicts are signposts, clearly pointing toward what's most important to each person around your table.

Remember, the goal is to nurture your family's relationships, honor everyone's unique contributions, and intentionally shape a legacy everyone can respect and embrace.

Real wealth is more than what you inherit. It's what you create from that inheritance. It's relationships strengthened, opportunities realized, and dreams and goals fulfilled.

> Real wealth is more than what you inherit. It's what you create from that inheritance. It's relationships strengthened, opportunities realized, and dreams and goals fulfilled.

If things feel uncertain or a little overwhelming right now, know that you're not alone. You're standing where countless other thoughtful, caring families have stood before you, many of whom benefited from the help of a neutral advisor who could facilitate clear, respectful communication and help uncover solid ground. But even with these practical steps to begin finding the best path forward, how do you ensure your decision aligns not just strategically, but also with the kind of life you genuinely want to build for yourself and your family?

The good news is you don't have to figure it all out today. Just start by getting clear on what matters most. The rest will follow.

HONORING VALUES
TO FIND SOLUTIONS

CHAPTER 4

The Land Values Framework: Making the Right Decision

Before Pat and I met with his family, we sat down for dinner so I could get a sense of his situation. During our meeting, I asked him a simple question: "What's your biggest challenge or your biggest goal as a landowner right now?"

He paused, his fork still in his hand. "I guess it's just trying to do the right thing."

"What's right *for you*?" I countered, pressing him a little.

He shrugged. "I don't know. That's the part I'm not sure about anymore."

This is often where most families get stuck. Not in the facts, but in the fog — the emotional gray area between what they feel, what they need, and what others are telling them they're supposed to do. The pressure from outside voices can be subtle, yet heavy, clouding the clarity families desperately need to find a decision that truly reflects their values, desires, and well-being.

"What I mean is, how do you define *the right thing*?" I asked. "Based on your values and your goals, what does a good outcome look like for you and your family?"

Suddenly, the look in Pat's eyes changed. Something had clicked.

"Oh! Well, I guess the right thing would be a situation where everyone is happy. Where we're not fighting. Where we all feel like we've made a decision we can live with."

"Okay," I said. "Now let's go one step deeper. What would make *you* happy? What are your financial goals? What kind of life do you want for yourself and your family? And what legacy do you want to leave behind as a farmer, and as a family man?"

That's when the answers started to come.

Pat told me about his plans for retirement and how he wanted to help send his grandkids to college. We talked about his family's history on the land and how he felt torn over this decision. "I feel like if we sell the farm, it will betray everything our parents and grandparents stood for," he said.

That's when I introduced Pat to something I now share with every family I work with: the LAND VALUES Framework.

We began to talk in detail about how Pat and the rest of his family viewed the value of the land and their own long-term goals and desires. Then, I said, "Pat, gathering together and acknowledging everyone's motivations are just the first two steps of the LAND VALUES framework. Once the cards are on the table, you can start deciding which values are most important to everyone and begin to look at the decision to keep or sell the farm through the lens of which option will help your family achieve those values."

Once Pat understood that gathering his family together to discuss their motivations, values, and desires would make the decision about what to do with the farm they'd inherited much easier, the conversation shifted profoundly.

Purely financial considerations like, "How much money can we get?" shifted to deeper, more meaningful questions like,

"How can this farm help us live the lives we truly want? Or would selling it bring us the life we dream of?"

Pat's all-or-nothing thinking changed from, "Does this decision honor our family?" to, "How can the decision we need to make best honor our family?"

The anxiety and fear about making the wrong decision faded, and clarity, confidence, and unity gradually emerged.

Money. Emotions. Inheritance. Long-standing expectations. It's a potent mix that can stir up old wounds, differing perspectives, and deep-seated fears. But even after understanding everyone's values and brainstorming possible solutions, a decision must be made about what to do with the land you've inherited. For some families, the best choice looks like one heir keeping the farm while others are bought out. For others, it looks like restructuring ownership or preserving part of the land through conservation. And sometimes, it means choosing to sell with a plan that honors what the farm has meant and who it made you.

Born from years of sitting at kitchen tables, listening to families navigate grief, pressure, love, and legacy, the LAND VALUES framework gives you a clear, human-centered path for making land decisions that feel financially sound *and* personally right. This practical, five-phase decision-making tool is designed to guide you through the emotional, financial, and generational layers of land ownership to identify the next right step for your family farm that honors both the past and the future.

UNDERSTANDING THE LAND VALUES FRAMEWORK

Think of the LAND VALUES framework as a structured conversation that moves your family from emotional gridlock to shared understanding and meaningful action. At the heart of the framework are the core principles that built rural America and likely built your family farm, too. Some families still live by these values every day, working tirelessly to sustain the legacy, while others are trying to rediscover them in the middle of grief, disagreement, or transition. Either way, these seven principles can be your compass again:

1. **Hard Work:** The everyday effort and sacrifices made by generations before you, and the ongoing dedication of the people on the land today.
2. **Resilience:** The strength to weather storms, both literal and figurative.
3. **Generational Sacrifice:** Respecting the tough choices and hard work of past and current generations to keep the farm healthy for the future.
4. **Faith:** A belief and trust in something greater — purpose, the land itself, continuity of life, or leaving a meaningful heritage.
5. **Stewardship:** Caring for the land not just for today, but for generations to come.
6. **Community:** A sense that your farm and the land play an important role in the larger community and landscape around you.
7. **Leaving Things Better:** The conviction that your greatest legacy might be what you leave behind for others.

These principles are the foundation of how land decisions are actually made. They're embedded in every acre, fencepost, and stone on your farm. They shape what matters to your family and are the reason it's hard to let go. As a result, families need a clear, straightforward way to assess their options and decide what to do with the land they've inherited.

Whether you're a fourth-generation farmer or a cousin who just inherited land you've never seen, these core principles give your family a common language for making a decision you can talk about openly and feel proud of years from now.

Here's how the five phases of the LAND VALUES framework work in practice. Think of it not as a checklist, but as a conversation map. One that can take your family from tension to trust, from stuck to moving forward.

The LAND VALUES Framework		
PHASE	**WHAT IT MEANS**	**YOUR NEXT STEP**
Phase 1: Listen	Understand each person's story, fears, and hopes.	Create space for open dialogue. Do not focus on solutions, just deep listening and reflection.
Phase 2: Acknowledge	Validate that the farm means different things to different people.	Identify the roles the farm has played financially, emotionally, culturally for each person.
Phase 3: Name Priorities	Use the 10 Land Values to bring to the surface what truly matters.	Work through each value area. Identify which are most important to whom and why.
Phase 4: Define Scenarios	Use your values to explore possible paths forward.	Discuss the real implications of keeping, selling, leasing, or restructuring ownership of the farm.
Phase 5: Strategize	Build a plan that reflects what matters most to your family.	Align on next steps, communicate clearly, and decide what to do with the land. Bring in help if needed.

These steps are simple, but not always easy. They work because they create space for truth, clarity, and action that reflect the best of what your family stands for.

Phases 1 and 2 of the LAND VALUES framework, Listen and Acknowledge, can sometimes be the most daunting steps. For some, getting their family in one room is an unimaginable scenario. For others, it's a regular Sunday afternoon. As illustrated by Pat's family in Chapter 3, taking the time to gather everyone around the table to have an honest conversation about their emotions, motivations, and goals can be an intense experience. But it's the necessary first step to gaining clarity around every stakeholder's true desires so you can move on to identifying the most satisfactory outcome.

Phase 3, Name Priorities, requires you to consider the 10 Land Values and identify the ones that are most important to you and your family. Think of these as lenses that help your family see the situation more clearly and completely. The goal of Phase 3 isn't to agree on all 10; it's to use them to understand different perspectives, find alignment, and identify your highest priorities. Sometimes it helps to rank these values. Other times, it's more useful to identify the top 2–3 that really matter most. You can access a free printable worksheet to help your family talk through these 10 value categories at AmericanFamilyFarmland.com/downloads.

The 10 Land Values include:

1. **Legacy and Lifestyle:** What traditions, memories, or daily rhythms do you want to preserve? How does your farm support the life you want to live and the story you want to continue?
2. **Alignment of Goals:** Does keeping or selling your farm line up with what your family is actually trying to do? Are you headed in the same direction or pulling apart without realizing it?

3. **Needs and Priorities:** What does each person in your family actually need financially, emotionally, logistically? Can those needs be met in a way that's fair and respectful by keeping or selling the farm?

4. **Decision-Making Structure:** How is your family communicating? Are decisions collaborative, respectful, and clear or reactive, rushed, or stuck?

5. **Value (Emotional and Financial):** Are you looking at the land's value from all angles — not just price per acre, but purpose, connection, and cost of ownership? Have you assessed these clearly to ensure your decisions make practical sense?

6. **Asset Management:** What's required to manage and maintain the farm today and tomorrow? Who has the capacity to manage, and who might need support?

7. **Long-Term Viability:** Is this farm set up to succeed across generations, or are there red flags to address now before they grow bigger? Are there clear benefits to selling or restructuring ownership now?

8. **Understanding Family Dynamics:** Have you had the hard conversations, or are assumptions leading the way? Do people feel seen or siloed?

9. **Environmental and Community Impact:** How does your decision ripple outward to impact the environment, your town, or future generations of farmers?

10. **Stewardship and Strategy:** Are you leading with clear intentions and a plan or reacting to emotion, urgency, or outside pressure?

Once you've identified your most important values, you'll have a much easier time understanding the real implications of keeping or selling the land you've inherited. And as a result, Phases 4 and 5, Define Scenarios and Strategize, become more about gathering a few clear options than getting stuck in a never-ending loop of asking "What if?"

CONNECTING LAND VALUES AND RETURN ON LIFE

As you move through the LAND VALUES framework, there's one mindset that makes every conversation more powerful: Return on Life. This lens is one that acknowledges the on-paper value of your land and focuses on what that value makes possible for your family. Essentially, Return on Life is the mindset that the right decision is one that supports not just your finances, but your well-being, your progress, and your freedom.

To keep it clear and meaningful, Return on Life focuses on three core components when making decisions:

1. **Well-being.** Does this decision bring your family closer together, or does it add stress and tension? Real well-being includes financial and the peace of mind and emotional harmony that come when you know your choices reflect your true priorities.

2. **Progress.** Does this choice move each member of your family forward in ways that matter most to them? Progress might mean educational opportunities for grandchildren, new entrepreneurial ventures, or simply the chance for family members to pursue their dreams without feeling anchored by obligations.

3. **Freedom.** Does this decision expand or restrict your family's options? For some, this might be the freedom to continue farming in a way that honors tradition. For others, it's the freedom to explore entirely new paths, unburdened by financial or emotional constraints. Freedom means being able to choose — not being locked into something that no longer fits.

When you thoughtfully combine the LAND VALUES framework and a Return on Life mindset, you unlock a powerful ability to clearly and confidently answer questions like:

- "If we keep the farm, will it genuinely enhance our family's well-being, or could it inadvertently cause more stress than it's worth?"
- "Does holding onto the farm help our family progress toward meaningful goals, or does it limit the opportunities available to the next generation?"
- "Does maintaining our land offer us the freedom to choose the lives we truly desire, or does it bind us to obligations that no longer reflect our family's reality?"

I've worked with families who were paralyzed by uncertainty and overwhelmed by guilt at the idea of selling their farm. Then they learned about the LAND VALUES framework and Return on Life mindset, and suddenly their decisions didn't feel like sacrifices. Instead, they felt authentic, empowering, and even joyful.

I've seen families choose to keep their farms, excited by the potential to pass down a thriving legacy enriched by innovation, sustainability, and shared purpose. Young family members who were introduced to regenerative farming practices or direct-to-consumer ventures, creating fresh opportunities that honor tradition while meeting new needs.

And I've seen other families choose to sell — not because they wanted to leave their history behind, but because the sale allowed them to unlock new possibilities. For these families, the proceeds became launching pads for education, entrepreneurial ventures, meaningful retirement, or creating charitable legacies honoring their ancestors' sacrifices.

In all scenarios, decisions made by using the LAND VALUES framework coupled with a Return on Life mindset bring relief, purpose, and satisfaction because families are able to maximize financial returns *and* genuinely reflect their deeper values.

WHAT'S BEHIND YOUR DECISION?

When you combine the LAND VALUES framework with a Return on Life mindset, decisions become less about pressure and more about possibility. You don't need to be perfect. You just need to be honest. And if openly discussing emotions and empathizing with different perspectives feels difficult or uncomfortable, that's completely normal and okay. Empathy is a skill, and like any skill, it can take practice and patience to develop.

This is exactly why many families choose to bring in a trusted advisor — someone neutral and experienced — to help facilitate these conversations. An advisor can ensure each person feels heard and respected and help create a safe, clear pathway toward mutual understanding and thoughtful solutions.

You don't have to navigate this complexity alone. Reaching out for support isn't a weakness; it's a wise and thoughtful step forward.

Remember, you don't have to get immediate agreement from everyone. You just need clarity, understanding, and respect for everyone involved, including yourself.

THE FRAMEWORK IN ACTION: 10 REAL-LIFE FAMILY SCENARIOS

To help bring the LAND VALUES framework and Return on Life mindset to life, I want to share ten real-world stories from families I've worked with. Each scenario captures a different set of tensions and illustrates thoughtful solutions these families found together.

As you read through these examples, you might recognize pieces of your own experience. Maybe one family's struggle mirrors your own, or perhaps another's solution sparks a new possibility you haven't yet considered. These stories aren't here to provide perfect answers; they're here to show what's possible when families take the time to clearly understand each other's values and perspectives.

1. The Legacy Divide: Balancing History and Financial Stability

When the Robinson siblings inherited their parents' farm, each saw the land differently. James was convinced that selling would dishonor everything their parents had worked for. Sarah, meanwhile, quietly worried about her children's financial future and believed the farm's value could secure it. Mark simply wished to avoid conflict and keep the family relationships intact. Initially, conversations were tense and emotional, leaving everyone feeling stuck.

To find common ground, they slowed down, listened openly to each other's underlying concerns, and brought in an advisor to facilitate. Doing so allowed them to craft a solution that honored James's desire to preserve the core of the family farm while carefully structuring a sale of some land, giving Sarah and Mark the security they needed. Their parents' legacy was protected, the family stayed connected, and each sibling felt genuinely respected.

2. The Fairness Dilemma: Recognizing Sweat Equity

Ben had dedicated his entire adult life to farming alongside his parents. Through every planting and harvest season, he'd been there, quietly building the farm's value with his labor, commitment, and sacrifice. When his parents passed away, he assumed the farm would become his (or at least, the majority of the farm), acknowledging the years of work he'd invested. Instead, the inheritance was split equally between him and his siblings, Anna and David, who hadn't been directly involved with the farm at all.

Ben felt betrayed. How could years of his hard work count for nothing more than equal shares with siblings who'd rarely set foot on the farm? David, dealing with personal financial pressure, urgently needed cash and wanted to sell. Anna felt caught in the middle and was simply hoping to maintain family harmony. Tensions grew, conversations stalled, and the family quickly became divided.

Rather than letting the resentment fester, my team and I helped Anna and David understand Ben's emotional pain and the practical reality of the time, effort, and resources he'd invested; the "sweat equity" and improvements that had *significantly* increased the farm's value over the years.

Together, they structured a solution recognizing Ben's unique contributions. They calculated and documented his years of effort, assigning real financial value to the countless hours he'd invested. This allowed Ben to *fairly* buy out his siblings and secure his farming future. David's financial needs were met, and Anna felt peace knowing fairness was achieved through respectful acknowledgment of each person's contributions.

3. The Paralyzed Partnership: From Frustration to Shared Purpose

Seven Miller cousins inherited their grandparents' farm, and while each cousin carried their own hopes and expectations, no clear leadership structure existed among them. As months passed without decisions, relationships frayed, the farm went fallow, and for two seasons it grew up in weeds.

Recognizing they were stuck, the cousins sought guidance and created space for open, structured conversation. Some met together while others needed to discuss the situation in a confidential setting. Eventually, they formed an LLC, clearly defined roles, and appointed a trusted farm manager. The land was revived, and a few cousins were bought out. Decisions started flowing clearly, and several cousins unexpectedly grew closer and built stronger relationships.

4. The Heir's Dilemma: Protecting the Legacy While Respecting Everyone's Needs

Jake Mitchell was deeply committed to farming. Every acre he worked held a lifetime of memories and meaning. But after his parents passed, Jake found himself in unfamiliar territory. His siblings, Tom and Lisa, saw the farm differently than he did. Tom faced immediate financial pressures and wanted to sell part of the property, while Lisa, having built a life elsewhere, preferred to step away entirely. Jake felt torn between honoring his parents' lifetime of work and preserving harmony within the family.

When we sat down together, we gently and openly talked through the realities each sibling faced. After clearly understanding everyone's priorities, we found a solution that thoughtfully balanced their needs. A partial land sale provided Tom with the financial relief he needed, Lisa achieved the resolution and closure she sought, and Jake secured the heart of the farm, allowing him to continue to live, breathe, and build upon the work his parents had started.

5. Avoidance to Action: A Family's Turning Point

When I met the Craig family, they were stuck, overwhelmed by years of silence, misunderstandings, and emotional strain following their mother's passing. Each sibling had a different view of what they wanted and what felt fair. Communication had all but broken-down, and the risk of losing the farm in a forced auction was growing by the day.

Over the course of a year, we worked carefully through the tension. One step at a time, I helped each sibling express their concerns, clarify priorities, and begin to trust the process. It wasn't easy. Emotions ran high, and progress was slow. But together, we stayed focused on the goal of honoring their mother's wishes and preserving the family's legacy.

In the end, the solution wasn't one-size-fits-all — it was thoughtful, creative, and fair. Two siblings chose to co-own and maintain the original home farm, working with a professional farm manager to ensure stewardship, stability, and peace of mind. The third sibling, who preferred more independence, became the sole owner of a separate parcel and now farms it himself.

This structure gave each person what they needed: resolution, ownership, and the ability to move forward on their own terms. One sibling told me, "For the first time in years, I feel at peace. We honored our mother, *and* we found a way forward."

Their story is a powerful reminder: with the right support, even the most complex family dynamics can lead to certainty, healing, and legacy.

6. The Sentimental Standoff: Protecting Memories While Facing Reality

Lisa's connection to the farm was deeply emotional. To her, every tree, fence line, the creek, and barn represented cherished family memories she couldn't imagine losing. Her brother, David, appreciated these memories but saw the farm's financial potential as an equally important priority. Their differences initially seemed impossible to bridge, and conversations quickly turned tense and defensive.

When we first sat down together, I carefully guided Lisa and David through their emotions and concerns. Rather than viewing their differences as irreconcilable, I encouraged them to consider and recognize that each of their viewpoints held genuine validity. Over time, we developed a solution that placed a deed restriction at the heart of the property, a wooded lot and a trail along the creek, protecting Lisa's treasured memories, while also identifying and selling a portion of the farm to meet David's clear financial goals for his family's future.

In finding this middle ground, Lisa and David discovered that sentimental value and financial practicality didn't have to oppose each other. Instead, their respectful compromise created an outcome both siblings could genuinely embrace.

7. The Forced Sale: Finding a Thoughtful Path Forward

When four siblings inherited their parents' farmland as tenants-in-common, they unknowingly stepped into a challenging situation. Under this ownership structure, any sibling could force a sale of the property, and that's exactly what happened. Facing personal financial pressures, one sibling felt compelled to trigger a forced sale. Immediately, the family's emotional connections and the future of the farm were thrown into crisis mode.

By the time they brought me in, tensions were high, and relationships were strained. Each sibling felt hurt, anxious, and uncertain about how to move forward. Recognizing the seriousness of the situation, I suggested bringing in an experienced attorney and a trusted CPA. Together, we formed a cohesive advisory team, allowing the family to fully understand the practical, financial, and legal complexities involved.

With careful guidance, we structured a solution that provided immediate financial relief for the sibling in need without forcing a sale of the entire farm. The attorney clearly outlined a buyout option that was fair and protective, while the CPA ensured the siblings understood all the financial and tax implications involved. Ultimately, the remaining siblings transitioned ownership into a family trust, providing clear guidelines and peace of mind for everyone.

This thoughtful collaboration not only protected their farmland but also allowed them to preserve *most* of their family relationships. By assembling a supportive team, the siblings successfully moved from a forced-sale crisis to a carefully planned resolution that honored everyone's needs, both practically and emotionally.

8. The Market Timing Dilemma: Balancing Opportunity with Patience

Farmland prices in the Heppner family's region were soaring, presenting what seemed like an ideal moment to sell. Some family members urged acting quickly to capture the market peak, anxious that missing this moment could mean significant financial loss. Others hesitated, believing patience would yield even better opportunities down the road. Emotions ran high as the urgency to decide created stress and tension within the family.

When I sat down with the Heppners, it quickly became clear that market timing wasn't their only concern. Beneath their differing viewpoints were questions about legacy, security, and what their family truly valued. We carefully evaluated the current market opportunities, weighing potential benefits against long-term family goals.

Together, we decided to hold a strategic farmland auction to capture immediate financial gains on a carefully selected portion of their land, while utilizing a 1031 exchange to reinvest in other real estate that better matched their long-term vision. The Heppners retained a meaningful part of their original farm, preserving family history and emotional ties, while clearly addressing financial objectives.

By approaching their decision thoughtfully and strategically rather than rushing into a sale, the Heppners learned that careful timing and thoughtful planning could secure their financial future while preserving the family heritage they valued most.

9. Retiring with Purpose: A Legacy that Lives On

When the Bradys first approached me for help, their concerns were financial and deeply personal. After decades of farming, they felt ready to retire, but the idea of simply selling their family's land and moving on felt incomplete. They worried that all the effort they'd poured into the farm might disappear once the land was sold. Their children had chosen paths away from farming, yet the Bradys still longed to see their farm remain productive and meaningful.

Together, we explored options beyond the typical choices of keeping or selling. After careful consideration, they decided to donate their farmland to a local foundation that aligned closely with their values of supporting farming practices focused on careful stewardship and long-term land health. The foundation leased the land to a local farmer who shared their commitment to stewardship, ensuring consistent income.

With guidance from their CPA and attorney, we structured an arrangement that supported the Bradys' financial goals and their desire for a meaningful legacy. Today, the ongoing rental income supports scholarships, mission trips, and local community initiatives important to their family. This balanced approach allowed the Bradys to achieve financial certainty, peace of mind, and a legacy that continues giving back, honoring both the tradition of their family's past and their hopes for the future.

10. Purposeful Farm Succession: Strategic Transitioning

As the senior generation of the Crawford family began to age, they recognized a pressing need for a clear succession plan.

Without it, their farm risked being lost to estate taxes or fragmented by competing family interests.

Their two children and their spouses held different visions for the family's estate. Kate and Brian, who actively farmed, were deeply connected to the land, and their livelihood was fully staked in the success of the family farm. Ellen and Mike, fully removed from farming, were focused on their own financial security and personal goals that required liquidity rather than land ownership.

Working closely with professional advisors, the Crawfords established a Family Limited Partnership (FLP). Brian and Kate became general partners, managing daily operations, while Ellen and Mike assumed limited partnership roles. This structure allowed the senior generation to gradually transfer ownership through annual gifting, leveraging valuation discounts to reduce taxes and protect the farm's value financially, operationally, and from a sense of principle and duty.

The FLP also included clearly defined buyout provisions to fairly compensate Ellen and Mike. Funded through structured payments and life insurance policies, this plan met their financial goals without forcing the sale of farm assets. Today, Brian and Kate continue the farming tradition, confidently managing the farm and grooming the next generation, while Ellen and Mike have achieved the financial freedom they desired.

YOU HAVE MORE OPTIONS THAN YOU REALIZE

Often, families say, "We just don't want to lose what this farm means."

When I hear this, I say, "You don't have to."

The LAND VALUES framework allows you to see that you don't have to hold onto your farm at all costs. It empowers you to make choices that truly reflect what matters most to you. Maybe that means keeping the land in your family and passing it to the next generation. Perhaps it means leasing the land to someone who respects your values and cares deeply for the soil. Or it could mean selling thoughtfully, strategically, and purposefully.

When family farms disappear, a piece of rural life vanishes with them. Yet, when families like yours make intentional decisions rooted deeply in both logic and legacy, that way of life doesn't vanish; it evolves. It thrives. And it continues forward.

Whether you're leaning toward keeping the farm, preparing for a careful sale, or still figuring things out, using the LAND VALUES framework alongside a Return on Life mindset can help you gain clarity about what's truly important, build confidence in your choices, and ensure your decisions align with your family's goals.

TAKE A MINUTE FOR SOME STRAIGHT TALK

Now, imagine you and I are sitting together at your kitchen table. Just like the meetings I've had with hundreds of families before you, this conversation is private and confidential. The coffee's on. The room is quiet. You finally have space to breathe and say what's really on your mind.

I'd look you in the eye and ask:

- "What does this farm mean to you, really?"
- "Are you carrying pressure to keep it that no one else sees?"
- "Do you feel stuck between honoring your legacy and protecting your peace?"
- "Are there people in your family that you're afraid to disappoint or conversations you've been avoiding for years?"

Then I'd ask the question I ask every client, sooner or later: "If we could fast-forward five years or 10 years, what does peace of mind look like for you?"

Maybe it's knowing your family still talks at Christmas. Maybe it's knowing the land went to a good steward. Maybe it's knowing you acted with integrity and made the best decision you could.

There's no "right" answer, but the best decisions, the ones that bring confidence and calm, come from understanding your emotions, your opportunities, and your options.

Fortunately, the frameworks, mindsets, and principles outlined in this book will help you find the answer that's right for you.

> The best decisions, the ones that bring confidence and calm, come from understanding your emotions, your opportunities, and your options.

CHAPTER 5

Financial Values: Opportunities for Your Best Life

"If we keep the farm, someone's going to be upset," Pat told me one day over dinner as we talked through the different considerations. "If we sell it, someone else will be upset. What am I supposed to do?"

That was the moment we started shifting the conversation from pressure to planning and from emotion to alignment.

I looked at him, feeling a pang of empathy for his dilemma.

"What's the middle ground here?" I asked. "What does everyone want beyond the numbers?

Pat paused to consider my questions.

"Some families are sure they want to sell, and they just need to know the strategy for getting the best sale," I said. "In your case, Pat, that's not decided yet. Based on the meeting we had with your family, everyone is still divided on whether to sell the farm or keep it.

"If you're looking to try and keep this farm, there are some pretty big questions to answer," I told him. "Have you been asking your family about their goals and how they want the memory of the farm to live on? The LAND VALUES questions that pertain to them?"

He nodded. "I have some of their answers, but I'm waiting for the rest."

"Okay, that's a start. Now, it's time to start thinking about the next phase of the framework and begin outlining possible scenarios for keeping and selling the farm. Since we're trying to determine whether keeping the farm has the potential to align with everyone's goals, we also need to look at the farm from a practical standpoint. The numbers will tell us whether keeping it's viable, or even possible. Once we have some hard data, you'll have a much better idea of whether you want to make that happen or go the route of selling."

Pat nodded. "That makes sense," he said. "Knowing if keeping the farm is a financially viable option will help everyone get clear about their priorities."

By now, you've spent some time reflecting on what your farm means to you emotionally, historically, and relationally. You understand the importance of the first three phases of the LAND VALUES framework and are ready to explore what keeping or selling your farm means financially. And more importantly, what it can *do* for your life today.

First, let's take an honest look at how your personal goals and financial needs line up with what your farm can realistically provide. Clarity comes when the life you're aiming for aligns clearly with your farm's financial realities. To show you what this looks like in practice, let's follow the story of the Taylors, a family navigating both tension and possibility.

Clarity comes when the life you're aiming for aligns clearly with your farm's financial realities.

A LIFE OUT OF BALANCE

Emily's mind drifted as she drove past endless fields along the familiar highway home, her windshield dotted with raindrops. The layoffs at her corporate ag company had doubled her workload, turning what was once a fulfilling career into pure exhaustion.

As she drove, she caught glimpses of the farms she'd frequently visited for work, where families laughed together, and kids ran free. *Why can't that be us?* she thought, a wave of longing and sadness tightening in her chest.

That evening, sitting at the kitchen table and the kids playing upstairs, her husband Jake sensed her dismay. "Rough day?" he asked.

"Yeah. I wish it was just today, though," she replied. "It seems like things have been going downhill a lot longer than that."

The silence hung between them. But Jake knew not to push. Whatever it was, she'd tell him when she was ready.

Finally, Emily looked across the table and asked softly, "Have you ever thought about moving back to the farm? It was hard work, but it always felt comfortable there. We were working toward something.

"And wouldn't you like Brayden and Olivia to grow up closer to family?" she added.

Jake's face tensed. Emily immediately regretted mentioning the farm, worried she'd added pressure to an already uncertain time.

But after a pause, Jake nodded. "Em, I've actually been thinking the same thing. I just didn't want to say it. But things on the farm aren't *that* good. Your grandpa and Brandon are barely breaking even. And with your job situation, I didn't want to throw another risk into the mix."

Emily looked away, frustration rising, "But there has to be another way. Right now, it's just the two of them. You and I are resourceful, Jake. With all of us working together, maybe there are ways we could make the farm more lucrative. And we wouldn't both have to quit our jobs. You still enjoy what you're doing, and with some belt-tightening, we could make it work. Shouldn't we at least consider what the alternatives might be?"

"Look, I don't want to burst your bubble," Jake said, reaching over to take her hands in his. "And I'd give anything to get you out of that job that's making you so unhappy and exhausted. Of course, we can think about it. Let's run it by your mom, brother, and grandpa and see what they think. Nothing will happen if we're not all on board. But maybe they'll like the thought of you being back home. They might even have some ideas of their own."

The weight in Emily's heart lightened a little as hope welled up. She gave Jake a small smile. "Thanks. That's a great idea."

Emily was voicing a hope many families carry quietly. The hope that maybe, just maybe, the farm could be more than a memory. It could be a solution.

CHRISTMAS AT THE FARM

The house smelled like pine and fresh bread, and familiar voices, stories, and laughter surrounded Grandpa Jim's kitchen table as everyone settled in for dinner. The whole family was home for Christmas, including Emily.

Except, she wasn't quite *there*. Her stomach churned as she looked around the table. The moment had to come.

Finally, she cleared her throat, breaking into the cheerful chatter.

"Jake and I have something we want to discuss. We've been talking about moving back to the farm."

Her brother Brandon looked up, his expression a mixture of surprise and worry. "Em, I'd love that. You know I would. But the truth is, the farm's barely supporting Mom, Grandpa, and me right now."

Emily nodded. "I know it's a risk. We wouldn't even consider it unless the whole family was on board. But I've been researching some ideas, and I think we can make the place more viable." She paused, then plunged in. "What if we renovated Grandpa's old barn into a wedding venue? Everything nearby is booked out months in advance. It could add a consistent income stream, something beyond grain."

Grandpa Jim cleared his throat, his voice strained. "Emily, seeing you and the kids every day would be wonderful. But I've already run the numbers and unless we sell the place, or part of it, I won't have enough to retire."

Brandon nodded. "Exactly. Unless someone can buy him out, there's not a realistic way forward."

A heavy silence fell across the table until Jake cautiously suggested, "Maybe we renovate slowly, keep costs manageable..."

Emily cut him off, shaking her head. "We don't have time. This isn't just about numbers; it's about our family, our future."

Brandon looked down at the table, his voice calm but firm. "It's not about dreams either, Em. It's about survival. I've seen too many farms go under chasing something that wasn't financially solid."

The silence returned, but Emily wasn't done hoping or fighting for the possibility of something better.

Like so many families, the Taylors weren't just navigating finances. They were navigating fear, identity, and the dream of building something that felt meaningful again.

DEFINE YOUR FINANCIAL GOALS

The first step in building a strategy is asking what financial success looks like for you and for everyone else at the table.

For the Taylors, that meant moving from short-term fears to long-term thinking. Could they pull together to create something more sustainable? Could they shift from reacting to building?

However, what the Taylors didn't realize was that their belief about the need to sell their farm was the result of focusing on the farm's capabilities and problems *at that moment* instead of thinking about the farm's long-term possibilities too. What if they could solve some of the current issues by pulling together and thinking creatively?

In cases like these, every decision potentially affects everyone. For instance, Emily, Jake, and Brandon could be putting Grandpa Jim's retirement at risk. But if they pulled it off, they could be setting him and the future of the farm up for a much better situation than he'd have if he just continued as he was. There were risks but also the potential of incredible rewards.

So, whether you're leaning toward keeping, selling, or reimagining your farm, you must define what the financial components of success look like for everyone and then see if you can find a way to make them happen in a way everyone will feel good about. Clearly defining financial success allows you to take the goals and values you identified in the first two phases of the LAND VALUES framework and map out possible scenarios for success and identify areas where you might need to adjust your expectations or desires.

This is the part where the spreadsheets do matter (but remember to keep it practical). You need a realistic idea of what your farm can financially support, and you'll need to work through the financials to make sure your ideas are viable. For instance, do you want to maximize cash flow now? Do you want to build long-term wealth for your kids? Do you want to protect your peace of mind or create new opportunities?

Your goals for your farm matter because they shape the strategy you'll need to implement to achieve financial success. As I've noted before, if you need immediate cash, selling might be the right choice. If you want long-term stability, leasing could provide steady income. If you plan to actively farm, you need to ensure cash flow, profitability, and sustainability.

Your goals for your farm matter because they shape the strategy you'll need to implement to achieve financial success.

As we see in both Emily's and Pat's situations, things get more complex when more than one person is involved because everyone has different goals. But even in these situations, you can still find a solution. The way to clearly understand possible scenarios that satisfy everyone's needs is by translating everyone's individual goals into financial outcomes and then working backward.

Emily's goal was clear: She wanted reconnection and a purposeful life for her family. To achieve this goal, she'd need to give up the income from her job and work to make the farm more lucrative to replace at least some of that lost revenue. For Jake, stability meant avoiding undue financial stress while focusing on long-term financial success. Brandon wanted to protect the existing operation without risky investments. And Grandpa Jim wanted to make sure he had the money to retire soon. They each had a unique vision for how the farm contributed to their Return on Life, and none of them were wrong.

Before we get too deep into the financials or investment comparisons, take a breath. You've read through stories. You've explored values. You've reflected on what matters most. Now it's time to get personal. Ask yourself these questions — not from a place of pressure, but from a place of purpose:

- Do I need immediate cash, or am I planning for long-term growth?
- Am I willing or able to sacrifice a little time or income to invest it in the long-term goals for the farm?

- How could we keep the farm viable in the short term yet add more income opportunities over the long term?
- What does financial *freedom* look like for me at this stage of life?

This is where your strategy starts. Your goals are the compass for understanding how to unlock the true potential of your land.

> Your goals are the compass for understanding how to unlock the true potential of your land.

DETERMINE HOW THE FARM CAN HELP YOU MEET YOUR FINANCIAL GOALS

Once your goals are clear, the next step of defining possible scenarios for keeping, selling, leasing, or restructuring ownership of your farm (Phase 4 of the LAND VALUES framework) is understanding whether your farm is financially positioned to support those goals.

This is where emotions and economics intersect. What you want may sound incredible, and yet, if it's not financially feasible, your dream can quickly turn into a nightmare. The following are eight key financial questions I walk through with farmers, heirs, investors, and families who are just trying to do the right thing.

You don't have to know all the answers yet, just start where you are.

1. Did You Inherit a Mortgage or Is the Farm Paid Off?

If you own your land free and clear, you're starting from a place of strength. It may generate solid rental income, appreciate steadily, and give you flexibility in how you manage it. But if the farm carries debt, it could create pressure. Monthly payments eat into profits. You may feel rushed to sell or unable to invest in improvements. For farming heirs, this can become a significant operational burden. In some cases, selling a portion of the land or refinancing might be the best path forward.

Ask yourself: Does keeping the land support my financial stability, or is it holding me back?"

2. What Are the Real Costs of Managing the Farm?

Owning land isn't the same as managing it.

If you're farming it yourself, you already know it's a lifestyle *and* a business. Inputs, equipment, labor, repairs, marketing, and recordkeeping all take capital, cash flow, and capacity.

If you're not farming, you still have decisions to make. Who's leasing the land? Are they paying market rent? Who's managing the lease or maintaining the improvements? Professional farm managers can help, but they typically charge five to 10 percent of gross income, and not all leases are created equal.

Ask yourself: Am I prepared to operate or oversee the farm as a business? If not, is it time to bring in help or explore a new direction?"

3. What's the Farm's Cash Flow Potential?

For many families, leasing the land is a great way to generate passive income. Fixed cash rent offers predictability while crop-share agreements offer more upside but also more volatility.

If you're actively farming the land, cash flow becomes a different kind of conversation. It's seasonal. It's variable. And it can be impacted by commodity prices, weather, supply costs, and yield. Even the best farmers face years where input costs skyrocket or revenue falls short. And in today's world, agriculture is facing one of the toughest economies in decades. If your life-style or retirement plan depends on steady income, leasing or selling might offer more alignment with your needs.

Ask yourself: Can I handle inconsistent income, or do I need predictable support?

4. Is the Land Appreciating and at What Rate?

Farmland tends to appreciate slowly and steadily, often outpacing inflation and offering strong long-term value. It's less volatile than the stock market, and hard assets are completely tangible.

That said, appreciation alone isn't always enough. The increasing value of your land also depends on:

- Location
- Productivity
- Drainage and infrastructure
- Water availability
- Proximity to markets, development, or conservation areas
- Your ability to maintain or improve the land

Ask yourself: Is my farm appreciating fast enough to justify holding it? Or could the value be better used elsewhere right now?

5. How Does Farmland Fit in Your Overall Investment Strategy?

This question is another opportunity for you to zoom out and look at the bigger picture. If you own other assets like stocks, real estate, or retirement accounts, how does the farm complement or complicate your existing portfolio? Farmland isn't liquid. You can't sell 10 acres tomorrow to cover a home repair. But it is stable and offers benefits like:

- Diversification
- Inflation protection
- Alternative revenue streams (hunting leases, agritourism, timber, CRP, etc.)

Still, if you're land-rich and cash-poor, it may be worth exploring a partial sale, refinance, or lease restructuring that creates more flexibility. This is why farming requires passion, a plan, and a safety net.

For those who are considering the continued operation of an inherited farm, it's critical to understand whether the current income is stable, growing, or hindered.

Ask yourself: Is the farm helping me build wealth or limiting my freedom to pivot, invest, or rest?

6. Should You Hold onto Farmland as an Appreciating Asset or Inflation Hedge?

Farmland has historically been a strong long-term store of value. When inflation rises, so do commodity prices — often increasing both farm income and land value. Add in improvements like drainage tile, irrigation systems, fencing, or soil conservation work, and your appreciation potential may increase even further. During economic uncertainty, that kind of consistency can offer real peace of mind.

But land value isn't guaranteed. And it's not the same everywhere. If your productivity and outputs are low, your drainage is poor, or the property lacks market access or diversity, appreciation may be slower than expected. Some landowners find that the farm's value has plateaued or that the costs to improve it outweigh the projected return. Holding for appreciation, a store of value, can be smart. But only when it fits your broader plan, not just your emotional attachment.

Farming requires passion, a plan, and a safety net.

Ask yourself: Do I have the time and flexibility to wait for those gains? Or could selling all or part of the land offer more meaningful progress today? Would unlocking the value now give me — or my family — more freedom and peace of mind?

7. How Does Farmland Compare to Other Investments?

Think of your farm as a puzzle piece. It doesn't give you the whole picture of your investment portfolio, but it's an important part of it. For many families, especially those who have other assets like retirement accounts or investment properties, farmland is a stabilizer. It's tangible, relatively low risk, and often tied to generational values. Unfortunately, it's also illiquid. You can't sell a few acres to cover an emergency. You can't easily rebalance it like a stock portfolio.

In some cases, families keep their farmland but diversify the *way* it's used. For example, they may explore:

- Alternative markets or relay cropping
- Timber sales, hunting leases, or agritourism experiences
- Easements or land preservation agreements
- Direct-to-consumer sales or CSA programs

Creative diversification can help the farm support multiple family members, even if only one is actively farming. But if you feel land ownership is limiting your financial freedom, don't be afraid to explore alternatives. Selling part, leasing differently, or reinvesting in a more flexible asset class might be the key to unlocking what you truly want.

Ask yourself: Is holding the farm giving me the balance I need, or is it keeping me from more flexible options? Would rebalancing my asset mix give me more freedom or opportunity?

8. Are You Taking Advantage of Tax Strategies?

Here's the good news: The right structure can make a big difference — not just in what you owe, but in what you keep, what you protect, and how confident you feel moving forward. This isn't about mastering tax law. It's about making smart, informed decisions with the right team beside you so your farm supports your life, not just your bottom line.

Farmland comes with unique tax opportunities if you're looking for them. I've seen families miss out on six-figure savings because they didn't have the right advisors asking the right questions early enough.

Here are a few key tools to understand:

- **1031 Exchange:** Allows you to sell and reinvest in another property without immediate capital gains taxes.
- **Step-Up in Basis:** Inherited land receives a new fair market value, potentially reducing future tax burdens.
- **Installment Sales:** Structured payments over time can ease tax implications and create predictable income.
- **Charitable Remainder Trusts:** A way to sell, support causes you care about, and reduce taxes.
- **Family Limited Partnerships** (FLPs): A structured way for families to manage farmland ownership and succession, preserving their legacy while reducing taxes and protecting assets.
- **Conservation Easements:** Reduce estate taxes while protecting the natural value of the land.
- **Depreciation Opportunities:** From qualifying equipment or improvements to bonus depreciation, there are multiple tax codes that can potentially be utilized to your advantage to offset income.

You don't have to become a tax expert (I am not a CPA, and this should not be considered tax advice), but you do need to have one on your team. How you sell or how you structure the ownership of your land can make a massive difference in what you keep, what you owe, and how your farm supports your long-term goals.

Ask Yourself: Do I have the right professionals guiding me through farmland-specific tax options? Are there overlooked opportunities that could better align with my goals? Have I evaluated how each option impacts my life today, not just my balance sheet tomorrow?

CREATIVE SOLUTIONS THAT WORK

The truth is that most families have more options than they realize. The key is to find a solution that reflects your values *and* your financial spreadsheet.

What Emily understood about her family's situation was that they had more options to increase the income and financial viability of their farm beyond traditional farming. Like the Taylors, you have more options than you think. Even when you feel stuck, you can often find creative ways to solve your issues if you really want to keep your farm. Here are a few real-life examples of creative, values-driven solutions that worked for my clients.

A Retiree's Passive Income Plan

James didn't want to farm anymore, but he wasn't ready to sell either. So, he hired a farm manager, ensured the lease had provisions for continual improvements, and turned his land into a passive income stream that supported his retirement and preserved his peace of mind. Today, he still visits the land, still walks the fields, and still calls it home.

The City Dweller Who Stayed Connected

Even though Sarah moved away long ago, the farm still pulled at her heart. Instead of selling the land, she leased the tillable acres to a young farmer, used a conservation easement to protect her woods and creek, and built a small cabin for quiet weekends with her friends. The land now provides income, biodiversity, and space to reconnect with nature.

The Family That Stayed Rooted

Maria and her husband wanted to be closer to their grandkids. Instead of selling the farm, they worked with an estate planner to create a trust, lease the land, and maintain a few wooded acres for their family to gather. Their grandkids now explore the same trails Maria once did, the lease supports retirement, and their family can stay connected.

Giving the Next Generation a Chance

Susan and Mark didn't farm, but their cousin Jake did. Rather than sell, they offered Jake a lease-to-own agreement, giving him a real shot at farm ownership over time without taking on significant debt up front. Jake grew his operation, stayed profitable, and eventually became the next steward of the land. For Susan and Mark, the best solution for them and their family wasn't about profit. It was about purpose.

FINANCIAL RED FLAGS TO WATCH OUT FOR

Not every farm is positioned for long-term success. Sometimes, keeping the land feels like the obvious choice, but sentiment alone won't sustain your operation long-term. Here are the red flags I tell families to look out for when they're comparing their goals and values with the financial realities of keeping or selling their farmland:

Lack of Financial Clarity

If your records about income, expenses, lease agreements, or property maintenance aren't clear and accurate, you're essentially flying blind. Without this critical financial clarity, you risk making decisions based on assumptions rather than facts. This can lead to unnecessary financial stress, family conflicts, or even long-term damage to the farm's value and legacy. Ensuring your financial picture is well-organized allows you to make informed decisions confidently, protecting both your family's financial security and emotional well-being.

No Recent Appraisal

Just because overall land values are high doesn't guarantee your farm shares that exact value. If it's been more than two or three years since your last professional appraisal or market analysis, you're missing critical information. An updated appraisal clarifies your farm's true market worth, empowering you to confidently negotiate leases, make strategic investment and operational decisions, plan estate transfers effectively, and maximize your farm's financial potential for both current and future generations.

Yield Declines or Soil Neglect

If your yields are flat or falling, it could be a sign of depleted soil, poor drainage, or an underperforming tenant. Generally, healthy soil equals healthy value, so if you hope to bring in top-dollar for your land, you need to have a clear understanding of what's happening beneath the surface.

A Tenant Who's Not the Right Fit

Are you getting fair market rent? Is the tenant transparent and proactive? If not, you may be losing money and future value.

Tensions Among Heirs or Co-Owners

If everyone isn't aligned on what to do with inherited farmland or if conversations keep getting delayed, long-term ownership may become more stressful than it's worth. Gathering your family together to begin discussing values and goals are the first two phases of the LAND VALUES framework and are the foundation of all future decisions to keep or sell your farm.

These aren't deal-breakers, but they are signals. With the right support, every one of them can be addressed, managed, or turned into an opportunity.

WHAT WORKS BEST FOR YOUR UNIQUE GOALS?

When it comes to finances, there's no one-size-fits-all answer — just the answer that fits you. Some families need liquidity now. Some want to preserve tradition. Others are ready to reimagine the farm entirely. Your goals, values, and financial needs should shape your next steps, so ask yourself:

- Am I keeping the farm because it supports my long-term goals?
- Is leasing or selling a better fit for my values, energy, and time?
- Is ownership helping me build the life I want or holding me back?

Your land is valuable. But *your life* is priceless. Make sure your farm is working for you, not the other way around.

Get the Free Checklist!

To make sure you've considered all the financial aspects necessary to make the right decision for your situation, the Eight-Step Decision Checklist is available as part of the Family Farm Values packet. This supplemental content is free for my readers! You can get it at AmericanFamilyFarmland.com/downloads.

Your land is valuable. But *your life* is priceless. Make sure your farm is working for you, not the other way around.

CHAPTER 6

The Family Legacy: Emotions at the Crossroads

Pat's family's emotional ups and downs didn't stop after our first family meeting. It had only been about a week since I'd sat with them around their kitchen table when, one morning, just as I was finishing a client meeting, my phone buzzed. It was Pat, and he sounded tired.

"Johnny," he said, "I'm still getting calls. Every few days, it's someone new. Linda says it's time to sell and move on. Josh wants to talk about conservation. Dan says he'll walk away if we don't keep the farm. I don't even know where to start anymore."

I could hear the weight of frustration and heartbreak in his words. He wasn't just trying to make a decision; he was trying to not let anyone down. This is what legacy often looks like in real life. It's the tension of many voices pulling in different directions, for different reasons.

95

I asked Pat to meet me at the diner just outside town. We grabbed a corner booth near the window and set our two steaming cups of black coffee between us. No pressure. Just space to talk.

After a few minutes of catching up, I said, "Pat, walk me through it. What's really going on with your siblings? What's *underneath* the arguing?"

He leaned back, eyes scanning the room as if trying to find the words in the wallpaper. "Well, Linda wants to use her share to help pay for college for her girls. I get that. Dan keeps saying Mom and Dad built this place for us to hold onto. Josh is all about keeping the soil healthy and wants to turn the property into some kind of regenerative farm. And Sarah... she just doesn't want the drama for her kids down the road."

I nodded slowly, then asked the question I knew would be hardest. "And what about you, Pat? Why do you want to keep the farm so badly?"

He looked down into his cup. "I don't know. I've been farming that ground since I was fifteen. It's who I am. I walk those fields, and I see Dad. I see Mom's garden. It's not just land; it's *who we are*. I don't want to lose that."

We sat in silence for a moment.

Then I said quietly, "I don't think you're fighting to keep the land, Pat. I think you're fighting to hold on to what your parents stood for. The way they lived. The meaning that place holds for all of you. I understand. The thing is, your siblings are doing the same thing."

He didn't say anything, but I could see the realization starting to land.

"They're not against you," I said. "They're just honoring what they value, which is security, peace, responsibility, and the sustainability of the farm. You're all carrying different pieces of the same story. The only difference is how you each currently view the next chapter. You each value different things."

Pat nodded, slowly. "So, what do I do?"

"You don't have to give up what matters," I said. "Let's think differently. Maybe it's time to redefine what honoring your parents could look like. What if you sold the farm to a local farmer who'll take care of it? Someone who'll walk those fields with the same respect you do. Could that still feel like honoring your parents?"

He looked away for a moment, then back at me.

"Yeah," he said. "If it goes to someone who'll take care of it — someone I trust — that'd feel different. I could live with that."

"Then that's your line in the sand," I said. "You're not saying yes to selling. You're saying yes to passing the baton."

Pat didn't make his decision that day. But something in him shifted. He stopped seeing the conversation about what to do with the farm as a battle to win and instead started seeing it as a bridge to build.

REDEFINING YOUR LEGACY

With this new perspective, Pat stopped asking "How do I get them to agree with me?" and started asking, "What if we sold to someone local who loved the land the way we do? Would that feel like honoring Mom and Dad? Could we preserve the stories, photos, and heritage so we pass down more than just acres? If we used part of the proceeds to support something meaningful like a conservation project, a scholarship, or a gift to a beginning farmer, would that still reflect who we are?"

With each question, his family softened. The tension gave way to curiosity. The debates turned into discussions. The land became less about possession and more about purpose.

Over the following weeks, Pat and I kept in touch. Sometimes it was a quick call after a sibling conversation. Other times, we'd meet in person in quiet spots away from group texts and generational expectations.

"You know," Pat said one afternoon, "I used to think I was the only one who really cared about the farm. But now I'm starting to see that everyone cares, they just express their feelings differently."

I nodded. "Exactly. And your job isn't to get everyone to see it *your* way. It's to listen for what they're really trying to protect."

One night, Pat called me after talking to Dan. "He told me he's scared," Pat said. "He's afraid that if we let go of the farm, we'll lose who we are."

"What did you say?" I asked.

"I told him I felt that way too." There was a pause on the other end of the line. "That landed for us both," Pat said quietly.

Then I asked him something I often ask families in this place: "What makes you who you are? The land itself, or the values you carry forward from it?"

I could tell the question stuck, though he didn't answer it right away. Later, Pat told me about a conversation he'd had with Linda. She'd been carrying a lot of guilt because she was afraid that advocating for a sale made her the "bad guy."

So, I asked Pat, "Do you think your mom and dad would want Linda to go into debt trying to keep the farm? Or would they want her to feel supported and safe?"

He paused. "They'd want her to be okay. They'd want *all* of us to be okay."

In another conversation, Pat shared how Josh, his youngest brother, had lit up when they discussed conservation options. "You'd invest in soil health regardless of the final decision?" Josh had asked.

"Of course," Pat said. "The land deserves that."

Even Sarah — who'd stayed quiet for months — opened up when Pat finally asked what she was afraid of.

"She's not disengaged," he told me. "She's just trying to avoid passing down a mess."

"She's protecting her kids," I said. "That's legacy, too."

"I hadn't thought of that," Pat admitted.

For years, Pat had thought of "legacy" as something solid and singular. Now, he realized it was layered. Personal. Evolving.

Linda wasn't greedy; she was practical. For her, legacy meant giving her daughters a better future. It meant college, stability, and options.

Dan wasn't just stubborn; he was deeply rooted. Legacy, to him, meant holding onto something tangible. Something you could stand on, walk across, and point to and say, "This is who we are."

Josh wasn't idealistic; he was visionary. He saw the land as something sacred. For him, legacy was about stewardship — healthy soil, clean water, regenerative practices, and preserving wildlife habitat for generations to come.

And Sarah? Sarah was the quiet one. But Pat saw her more clearly now. She wasn't avoiding the family. She was trying to protect her kids from inheriting conflict. For her, legacy meant simplicity. Harmony. A clean slate.

Inheriting a family farm means stepping into a story. The barns, the fencerows, the woods and creeks, and the old farmhouse are sacred spaces where memories live. The land becomes an identity. It becomes home, even if you've moved away. That's why any change — transitioning ownership, exploring new uses, deciding whether to sell — can feel emotional, complicated, and even paralyzing.

Fortunately, the LAND VALUES framework provides a clear process for naming these emotions, evaluating your values, and then defining scenarios for keeping or selling your farm that honor your family.

So, if you've identified family legacy as your most important value, you're not just deciding what to do with land, you're deciding what kind of story your family will tell next. If you're feeling stuck, start by asking:

- Have conversations about the farm become emotionally charged, or are we avoiding talking about what to do next altogether?
- Are different family members pulling in different directions?
- Do I feel pressure to keep the farm or guilt at the thought of letting it go?
- Are decisions being delayed because no one wants to be the one to speak the truth?

THE MEANING AND PRESSURE OF FAMILY LEGACY

Families often feel pressure to keep the farm at all costs because they believe that to sell or change anything is to betray previous generations. If this is you, know that you're not alone. Yet, sometimes we mistake the physical form of a legacy for the true essence behind it. The farm was how your parents lived out their values. But hard work, generosity, grit, and love don't live in the soil. They live in you. Legacy isn't a contract. It's a gift. And sometimes the most respectful thing we can do with a gift is use it wisely, especially when the giver isn't here to guide us anymore.

Pat felt that pressure deeply. One evening, he called me, and I could hear the fear in his voice. He wasn't panicked, just quiet.

"I keep thinking about Mom and Dad," he said. "How proud they were to pass down the farm. And now? If we let it go, it feels like I'm betraying them."

I let that hang for a moment, then said, "Pat, what do you think they really wanted? For you to hold the deed or for you to live a good life?"

He didn't say anything right away, so I continued. "Sometimes we confuse the *form* of legacy with the *feeling* of it. The farm was how your parents lived out their values. But hard work, generosity, grit, and love don't live in the soil. They live in you."

Once again, that landed.

The next time Pat spoke with his siblings, he approached the conversation differently. Instead of defending the farm, he asked:

"Would Mom and Dad want our kids to inherit a conflict or a clean, clear path?"

"What if honoring our parents means making a decision that protects *us*, too?"

"If we let go of the land but hold onto our family's long-standing values, what could that make possible?"

Pat stopped fighting to keep the land and started learning how to carry the fundamentals of their family's heritage forward. He discovered that legacy isn't about never letting go. It's about knowing what's worth holding onto and what it's finally okay to release.

SITUATIONS CHANGE, BUT VALUES LIVE ON

By early spring, the snow had melted, the fields were softening, and the calls from Pat had slowed. The pressure Pat had felt to

Legacy isn't about never letting go. It's about knowing what's worth holding onto and what it's finally okay to release.

make the right decision was gone because now he wasn't holding the weight alone.

The next time we met was at the edge of one of the fields he'd worked for decades. The trees were still bare, and the wind was still. The air was filled with the kind of quiet that comes with clarity.

"Johnny," he said. "What if we do sell? What if we let go of the land and it ends up being the best decision for everyone except me?"

After a moment, I said, "Pat, legacy grows. It adapts. It's not about perfection; it's about integrity."

I looked at him and added, "Your parents didn't just leave you land, they left you resilience, love, sacrifice, and family. Maybe the real gift is learning how to carry that forward even when the details change."

Pat nodded and said, "Maybe preserving legacy is about making hard choices for the sake of what's best, like Mom and Dad always did."

In the weeks that followed, we started working on a new plan — one that reflected his family's values, not just the value of the family's land. We explored selling the farmland to a local farmer who shared their conservation values. We allocated the proceeds of the sale to fund a local scholarship in honor of Pat's parents. And we marked out a wooded section near the creek that was home to deer, pollinators, and childhood memories that would be preserved through a conservation easement.

Over the years, I've sat at hundreds of kitchen tables. I've walked past barns, creeks, rows of crops, wildlife at the woods edge, and rural grave sites and headstones. I've listened to heirs contemplate how their decision will impact their family's history and heritage as they whisper the same questions you may be asking right now:

"If we sell, are we turning our back on everything our parents worked for?"

"If we keep it, are we forcing the next generation into something they didn't choose?"

"Is there a way to make a decision that feels fair, peaceful, and purpose-driven?"

The answer to all these questions is *yes*, but only when you slow down enough to ask the right questions about your values, financial goals, and what honoring a family legacy means to you. So, before you make the decision to keep or sell your farm, consider the following questions:

- Can this land help create the life I need, or are there smarter ways to use its value?
- Can I honor my family's history even if ownership changes?
- Can I protect the land through conservation, lease structures, or a thoughtful sale?
- Does tradition live in ownership or in the values that carry on through my choices?
- Can our legacy live through story, generosity, or community impact?
- Can I help a younger farmer begin even if my family doesn't continue to farm?
- Could my family's land still protect habitat, pollinators, or clean water even in new hands?
- Will my decision bring clarity and freedom to the next generation?

To help your family sort through emotions, opportunities, and values, use this table as a starting point for discussion.

Core Value	Value in Practice	Legacy Beyond Ownership
Financial Security	Selling to support retirement, reduce financial strain, or invest in what matters most.	Peace of mind. Stability. A chance to redirect energy toward life, not just land.
Stewardship	Caring for the land with intention through conservation, crop rotation, cover crops, livestock integration, or simply farming it well.	Easements, long-term leases with stewardship goals, or partnerships that preserve productivity and natural resources.
Heritage and Tradition	Family stories, old barns, and rural values passed through generations.	Sharing stories, preserving photos, passing down heirlooms, or naming a scholarship in their honor.
Family Harmony	Clarifying roles to reduce future conflict, confusion, or emotional stress.	Trusts, LLCs, FLPs, buy-sell agreements, or guided succession planning.
Community Impact	Keeping land in local hands or supporting future farmers.	Affordable leases, local scholarships, ag incubators, or land access initiatives.
Emotional Clarity	Releasing guilt, pressure, or expectations that no longer fit your family's reality.	Values-based decision-making. Peace of mind. A fresh chapter rooted in integrity.

Redefining Your Family's Legacy

To help spark conversation about what honoring and preserving your family's legacy means to everyone involved in the decision to keep or sell your inherited farmland, use the *Redefining Your Family's Legacy* reflection worksheet available for free at AmericanFamilyFarmland.com/downloads.

CHAPTER 7

Community Values and American Agriculture: When Your Personal Legacy Meets the Greater Good

In the previous chapters, you've explored the power of clarifying your family's emotional values, navigating tough decisions, and aligning your choices with meaningful, long-term goals. But what happens when your family's decisions reach beyond your own fence line?

Your farm is part of your local economy, rural traditions, and regional conservation efforts, and is often the heartbeat of the community around you. The decisions you make about your farm ripple outward, impacting local jobs, schools, wildlife, and neighbors who've become family over generations.

This is why one of the biggest emotional factors to reconcile when deciding whether to sell a farm is often about steward-ship. I've sat with countless farm families who've quietly said:

"Johnny, I can't bear the thought of the land being developed or paved over."

"We've got an offer, but do they really understand what it means to care for this land?"

"Our farm is more than soil, woods, livestock, or acreage — it's generations of sacrifice and responsibility."

In this chapter, we'll carefully examine what's truly at stake when you consider your farm's role in the broader community. My goal is not to overwhelm you with responsibility, but to empower you with clarity. As with our discussion about reframing legacy in Chapter 6, it's possible to honor stewardship as your most important value, whether you keep, lease, or sell your inherited farmland.

Let's first explore why land stewardship matters now more than ever.

THE SHIFTING LANDSCAPE OF AMERICAN FAMILY FARMING

You've probably noticed the familiar farms along the highway being replaced by subdivisions or warehouses. Maybe you've driven past an old neighbor's place and felt a pang of loss when you saw bulldozers instead of barns. These changes reflect a deep shift in rural America. Every single day, we lose roughly 2,000 acres of farmland to development.[2] That's not just acres

---

2 Sallet, Lori. "NEW REPORT: Smarter Land Use Planning Is Urgently Needed to Safeguard the Land That Grows Our Food." American Farmland Trust, June 29, 2022. https://farmland.org/blog/new-report-smarter-land-use-planning-is-urgently-needed-to-safeguard-the-land-that-grows-our-food.

disappearing; it's the erosion of our rural heritage, family traditions, and local economies. It's schools losing students, businesses closing their doors, and towns losing the heartbeat that keeps them alive.

This isn't happening because people stopped caring; it's happening because keeping a family farm viable is tougher than ever. With the average American farmer nearing retirement and fewer young people stepping in to take their place, there's often no clear successor to take over the stewardship of the land when it comes time to pass the torch.

Maybe you've felt this yourself, wondering, *Will anyone care for this land as deeply as my family did?* or, *If we sell, what does that mean for our community?* Yes, there are practical details that need to be considered, but these concerns are deeply personal. They speak to your values, your family's story, and your role in the community's future.

Understanding this bigger picture about the value of preserving rural land doesn't have to overwhelm you. Instead, let it empower you. You have more influence over your farm's local impact than you may realize. The choices you make about your land today can help preserve rural life, protect community values, and ensure your family's values continue long after your name leaves the deed.

WHO'S REALLY BUYING YOUR LAND?

One of the most frequent questions I'm asked by landowners is, "If we sell, who's going to end up with the land?" It's a fair question because the reality is that farmland buyers aren't always neighbors you grew up with or even people who share your values. Increasingly, farmland across the United States is being bought by investment firms, corporate entities, and foreign investors. Right now, foreign investors own more than 45 million acres of American farmland.[3] A total area that's bigger than the state of Iowa.

Why does this matter to you and your community?

When farmland changes hands, it can profoundly shape the future of your community. Some new owners will share your dedication to responsible stewardship, sustainability, and local traditions. Others may approach farmland primarily as a financial asset, prioritizing appreciation, profitability, or future development over community or conservation goals.

That's why it's important to look beyond the offer price and ask the right questions. Who is this buyer? What are their intentions? And will they honor the same care, stewardship, and commitment to community that your family has invested in over generations?

You might be thinking, *Why does this affect me?* It's important to understand who you're selling to because when land transitions away from local, hands-on ownership, the ripple effects can be dramatic. Local tenants may be displaced. Conservation and stewardship practices can fall by the wayside. The businesses your farm supported — local mechanics, restaurants, and even schools — may feel the impact.

Of course, not all investment-driven purchases are harmful. Many buyers do prioritize responsible practices and community involvement. But without clear intention and careful decision-making from families like yours, stewardship can quickly become secondary. This doesn't mean you shouldn't sell. It means your choice about *who* to sell to matters.

3   Munch, Daniel. "Foreign Footprints: Trends in U.S. Agricultural Land Ownership." American Farm Bureau Federation, January 14, 2025. https://www.fb.org/market-intel/foreign-footprints-trends-in-u-s-agricultural-land-ownership.

So, before you decide if selling is the right option for you, ask yourself:

- Who do I trust to care for this land the way my family has?
- What values do I want reflected in the next chapter of this farm?
- How can my decision strengthen my community?

Your answers will guide you toward buyers who view your land as more than an investment opportunity. They'll guide you toward a decision that honors your family's heritage, protects community values, and preserves the land you love.

Now, let's look even closer at the hidden community impacts and opportunities your farmland decisions create.

THE FARM'S ROLE IN YOUR LOCAL ECONOMY

If you've ever visited a small town where the businesses have quietly closed, the schools have fewer students, and the community events feel just a little emptier each year, then you've witnessed firsthand the hidden cost of family farms disappearing. When your farm thrives, it sustains:

- The downtown shop owners who rely on local business
- The veterinarian who tends to livestock and contributes to the vitality of the local community
- The small-town grocery store, café, or gas station that survives because local families shop, eat, and fuel their vehicles there
- The schools, churches, and community centers whose lifeblood is the families who live, work, and grow up on these farms

But when a farm transitions away from agricultural use — especially when it's purchased by someone disconnected from the community or converted for development — those relationships start to fray.

When families like yours consider selling or transitioning farmland, you hold a rare and valuable opportunity to protect local traditions and livelihoods by carefully choosing who farms the land next; to invest in your community's future by selling or leasing to local farmers, young families, or organizations committed to responsible stewardship; and to maintain local agriculture and rural vitality by exploring strategies like community foundations, farm preservation trusts, or beginning farmer programs.

As you think through your own choices, ask yourself these important questions:

- Who can best carry on the legacy and values of my farm?
- How can I ensure my decisions help rather than harm local businesses, schools, and families?
- What does responsible stewardship look like in practical terms for my community?

Remember, selling your farm doesn't mean you're stepping away from stewardship. It means you have a unique chance to ensure the land and everything it represents continues to benefit your community, long after your name is off the deed.

By now, you've considered the values outlined in Chapter 3, adopted a Return on Life mindset to view your farm through a lens that considers both your short and long-term goals, and used the LAND VALUES framework to gain alignment within your family so you can make a decision that best supports everyone involved. If land stewardship is at the top of your list of values, considering *who* will purchase your land is a smart strategy that honors what's important to you and serves the future of your community and rural America.

Next, let's explore how practical stewardship decisions today can ensure that your family's heritage and your community's well-being are protected for generations to come.

CHOOSING VALUES OVER CONVENIENCE

Over the years, I've talked with many families like yours who are quietly wrestling with how to be good stewards of the land they've inherited, even if they've decided that selling is the best option for them. They often ask themselves the same questions you're probably asking now:

- Who will care for the farm when I'm no longer here?
- Will the new owners value this land as deeply as my family has?
- Am I protecting what matters most or simply avoiding tough decisions?

Stewardship is rooted in questions like these because landowners often care deeply about how they treat the land and how to thoughtfully choose its future caretakers. But if we think about stewardship practically, it can mean choosing to work with tenants who actively care about preserving and improving the topsoil, habitat, or wildlife corridors, and community responsibility. It can mean maintaining and documenting your farm's improvements, tile and drainage records, crop or livestock rotations, soil fertility, and historic yields, or writing out your next set of improvement goals so future caretakers know exactly how to protect and build upon your legacy. It can mean selecting buyers or future operators who share your values and appreciate the responsibility that comes with owning farmland.

It's important to acknowledge that good stewardship is not exclusive to any single farming method. Both conventional and regenerative agricultural practices can, and do, play a valuable role in responsible farmland management. The best stewardship approach depends on your land's unique circumstances, your family's values, and your community's needs. Practicality, adaptability, and respect for diverse farming traditions are essential.

Maybe stewardship means enrolling in a conservation program, setting up a longer-term lease arrangement with a trusted local farmer or family member, or considering a farmland easement that permanently protects your land from development. Maybe it simply means thoughtfully structuring your transition to ensure your farm continues to support local families and community businesses through a local foundation.

No matter how you define stewardship, ultimately it's about preserving legacy and fostering clear intentions. It's about knowing that your legacy isn't measured in how long your name remains on the land, but in how thoughtfully you prepare it for the generations to come.

As you consider what stewardship means to you, ask yourself these key questions:

- Am I actively planning for the long-term health of this land?
- Are the decisions I make today aligned with what I want my legacy to be?
- Am I prioritizing stewardship clearly or simply reacting to short-term pressures?

Now, let's explore how responsible stewardship translates directly into practical value.

PROTECTING YOUR HERITAGE AND YOUR COMMUNITY

Honoring stewardship as your most important value begins with understanding a fundamental truth: Stewardship isn't about control; it's about continuity. Whether you're actively farming, leasing your land, or considering a sale, you have an opportunity to influence how your farm is managed long after your family steps back from the daily work.

I've worked with families who deeply worry about the future of their farms. They say things like:

- "If we sell, how can we know our land will stay productive?"
- "Who will care for the wildlife habitats or the soil health that took decades to build?"
- "How can we protect what generations have worked so hard to create?"

These deeply personal and practical questions speak to the heart of what farmland stewardship truly means.

Many families deeply worry about the future of their farms. Sometimes, this worry prevents them from taking action to sell or reimagine how their inherited land is used, and they end up in situations full of stress, family discontent, or financial hardship. In these situations, I gently remind them that good stewardship means making intentional choices that prioritize long-term health and community vitality. It involves actions like:

- Choosing tenants or buyers who share your family's values and land ethic.
- Exploring agricultural easements or deed restrictions that permanently protect your farmland from future development.

- Encouraging and documenting sustainable practices, such as cover cropping, no-till farming, buffer strips, and habitat conservation.
- Ensuring infrastructure like tile, fences, roads, and barns remains in good repair so future caretakers can manage the land effectively.

You don't have to be a hands-on farmer to practice great stewardship. You simply need clarity, intention, and the willingness to ask the right questions. Start by considering the following:

- What do I want my land to look like 20, 50, or even 100 years from now?
- How can I ensure the next generation cares for the land as deeply as we have?
- How can my decisions today protect my community tomorrow?

Well-stewarded farms attract better tenants, stronger offers, and higher values. They sustain thriving communities. They protect wildlife, soil, and water resources. They carry forward your family's story in a meaningful way. So, before you make the decision to keep, sell, or reimagine your farm, remember that stewardship is about passing the land on in a way that honors your family's legacy, your community's future, and the integrity of the land itself.

If you're feeling the weight of all these considerations, you're not alone. The purpose of this chapter isn't to overwhelm you or place more pressure on your shoulders; it's to remind you that you have options. Stewardship can take many forms, and you don't need to do everything at once.

Legacy is built not by controlling the outcome, but by planting the right seeds.

You simply need to take one intentional step forward that's aligned with your values, your goals, and your family's vision for the future. Legacy is built not by controlling the outcome, but by planting the right seeds.

GOOD STEWARDSHIP EQUALS GOOD VALUE

Let's talk openly about something every farmland owner should understand clearly: Good stewardship is financially smart.

You've likely felt this intuitively. You've seen how farms that maintain soil fertility, practice soil preservation, have diversified income and risk management practices, and keep infrastructure strong consistently produce higher yields and ROI, attract better tenants, command higher rents, and generate stronger market interest. Fortunately for us, there's plenty of data to support these outcomes. Multiple studies from leading universities and agricultural groups have confirmed that farms emphasizing good stewardship practices often sell at premium prices and hold their value better during market downturns.[4]

Here's what stewardship looks like from a financial perspective:

- **Higher Market Values:** Documented fertility, soil health, well-maintained infrastructure, and management practices can significantly enhance your land's market value, whether you're actively farming or considering an eventual sale.

---

4 Ribaudo, Marc. "Creating Markets for Environmental Stewardship: Potential Benefits and Problems." USDA Economic Research Service, September 1, 2008. https://ers.usda.gov/amber-waves/2008/september/creating-markets-for-environmental-stewardship-potential-benefits-and-problems.

- **Stronger Tenant Relationships:** Landowners who empha-size stewardship attract tenants invested in the farm's long-term value, resulting in better maintenance, longer leases, and mutual trust. Similarly, farmers benefit from secure arrangements that reward their commitment to land care.

- **Enhanced Productivity and Yields:** Practices like nutrient or manure management plans, reduced tillage, cover cropping, and sustainable grazing can improve the land and often lead directly to increased productivity, benefiting active farmers with higher yields and landowners with more attractive income potential.

- **Reliant, Sustainable Income:** Stewardship-driven farms typically generate consistent returns year after year, providing farmers with stable operational income and landowners with dependable rental income, while maintaining the farm's overall financial viability.

- **Resilience During Downturns:** Farms managed with stewardship practices such as diversified income, proactive risk management, healthy soils, varied cropping systems, and efficient water management are often more resilient in agricultural downturns. These practices buffer against drought, economic uncertainty, and commodity price volatility, stabilizing land values and financial performance.

Remember, stewardship is not defined by labels like "conventional" or "regenerative." Effective stewardship includes all practices that protect soil health, maintain productivity, conserve natural resources, and responsibly manage the land for future generations. Whether your farm follows conventional agricultural methods, regenerative approaches, or a balanced combination of both, your intentionality and thoughtful management are what truly matter.

The market now rewards farms managed with clarity and purpose. Buyers today want proof, not promises. They seek farms that tell a story of responsible care, managed risk, consistent productivity, and meaningful investment. Simply put, stewardship translates your family's values into tangible, measurable value. It ensures that your family's work is not only preserved but also strengthened, enhancing your financial security and community standing along the way.

> **Stewardship translates your family's values into tangible, measurable value.**

As you continue thinking about your farm's future, keep these questions in mind:

- Am I clearly documenting and communicating the stewardship practices we've used?
- How can better stewardship now translate into stronger financial outcomes down the road?
- Are my current tenants aligned with my stewardship values and long-term vision for the land?

By making stewardship a core element of your strategy, you're actively enhancing your land's financial value and personal meaning. But beyond increasing the value of your land, how does good stewardship impact the next generation of farmers who will ensure your land continues to thrive?

CONNECTING YOUR FARM TO THE NEXT GENERATION

One of the toughest realizations for many farm families is understanding that their own children or grandchildren might not be the ones to continue farming. But this doesn't mean your family's stewardship legacy has to end.

Right now, all across America, a dedicated and passionate generation of young farmers is ready to step up. They're skilled, innovative, and committed, but they often lack access to land. As a current landowner, you hold something incredibly valuable to them: *opportunity.* Bringing on younger, not-yet-established farmers allows you to develop values-driven relationships built on mutual trust and shared commitment to responsible stewardship.

When you help a young farmer get established, you're killing two birds with one stone. Yes, you're entering into a transactional relationship, but long-term leases, mentorship agreements, or gradual ownership transfers that reflect your values and support your personal goals, all while fostering the next generation's success, are your chance to extend your most important land values you identified in Chapter 3.

Consider these questions as you reflect on connecting your farmland with the right next-generation steward:

- Who do I trust to honor my land, community, and personal values and continue the work my family started on this land?
- How can connecting with a beginning farmer benefit my community, my family, and my personal Return on Life?
- What creative arrangements might best support the goals of both our family and the new farmers stepping forward?

By connecting your land with the right next-generation caretaker, you ensure that your family's legacy of stewardship and values will be carried forward by capable and committed hands, benefiting your land, your community, and generations to come.

AGRICULTURAL CONSERVATION EASEMENTS AND DEED RESTRICTIONS

One of the most effective methods available to protect your farmland is an agricultural conservation easement or deed restriction. These tools can prevent your farmland from being paved over, subdivided, or converted for non-agricultural or non-habitat purposes. *While not the right fit for every family,* easements and restrictions can be a powerful option for those who want long-term protection and are comfortable with the complexities and implications involved, such as:

- **Permanence:** Conservation easements are generally permanent and binding. Once established, the restrictions on land use typically cannot be reversed or significantly altered. This means that future generations will inherit these restrictions, which could limit their flexibility and decision-making.

- **Financial Commitments (Stewardship Endowments):** Establishing a conservation easement usually involves creating a stewardship endowment or fund. This financial reserve is required to ensure ongoing management, monitoring, and enforcement of the easement's conditions. This represents a significant financial responsibility that your family must be prepared for.

- **Loss of Flexibility and Future Land-Use Options:** Conservation easements and deed restrictions explicitly limit or prohibit activities such as property subdivision, residential or commercial development, and sometimes certain agricultural practices. These limitations permanently reduce future flexibility and can affect marketability, property values, and liquidity.

- **Financial Implications and Market Value Impact:** While easements can offer significant tax incentives

122

or upfront financial benefits, they typically decrease the land's overall market value due to reduced future uses. It's critical that you fully understand and evaluate these financial trade-offs before entering into an agreement.

Given these complexities, it's essential to seek detailed guidance from professionals who specialize in conservation easements and land stewardship. Before finalizing decisions about conservation easements or deed restrictions, consult closely with a qualified agricultural conservation attorney, land advisor, and financial professional. Their expertise will help you clearly understand long-term implications, avoid unforeseen challenges, and ensure your decisions fully align with your family's financial, emotional, and community values.

Still, here's how agricultural easements and deed restrictions can be practical benefits for you and your family:

- **Permanent Protection:** Ensure your farmland remains farmland, wildlife habitat (or a combination of both) indefinitely, preserving the hard work and dedication your family invested.
- **Financial Benefits:** Take advantage of valuable potential financial incentives, including tax breaks or compensation from conservation groups.
- **Stewardship Assurance:** Give yourself peace of mind, knowing that the land you love will remain productive, healthy, and supportive of local agriculture and wildlife habitats for generations to come.
- **Community Impact:** Preserve the rural character, local economies, and small-town life that your farm actively supports.

Many families feel profound relief once these protections are in place. Instead of worrying about what might happen, you can focus on confidently shaping what *will* happen, securing your vision of stewardship for generations.

To evaluate if conservation easements or deed restrictions might align with your vision, consider questions like:

- Do I want to permanently safeguard my farm from future development pressures?
- Would the financial incentives or compensation associated with these agreements support our family's personal or retirement goals?
- How important is it to me to leave this land better off for the next generation, regardless of who eventually owns it?

Most importantly, ask yourself: "Am I comfortable with the permanence, limitations, and financial responsibilities associated with a conservation easement or deed restriction?"

By taking these proactive steps and clearly understanding their long-term complexities and implications, you'll ensure your land continues to reflect your family's deeply held values and goals without leaving the future up to chance.

PRACTICAL STEPS FOR GOOD STEWARDSHIP

Now that I've shared several key ways you can ensure the stewardship of your land even if you're not the one actively farming, here's a quick summary of proven and actionable strategies that many farm families use to protect their land's health and productivity long-term:

1. Choose the Right Tenant or Buyer

Your farm's future depends heavily on who farms it next. Whether leasing or selling, look beyond who offers the most money. Prioritize individuals or families who align with your stewardship values, embrace similar management practices, or have strong community ties.

2. Agricultural Conservation Easements and Deed Restrictions

Powerful legal tools like conservation easements and deed restrictions permanently protect your land from future development. Easements can preserve cropland, pasture, woodland, waterways, and wildlife habitats. They can even offer significant tax incentives or compensation, allowing you to honor your values while protecting your financial security.

3. Document and Share Farm Records

Buyers and tenants who share your values will deeply appreciate clear records of yield history, soil and organic matter tests, management practices, grazing patterns, maps, and improvement details. Well-documented farms command stronger offers, attract better tenants, and retain their value more effectively.

4. Maintain Infrastructure Proactively

Healthy farms require working infrastructure assets like drainage tiles, fencing, buildings, and roads. Prioritize maintenance to protect property value and ensure future stewards can effectively, profitably, and sustainably manage the land in the future.

5. Invest in Stewardship Practices

Many families choose practices aimed at improving soil health, protecting water quality, and strengthening long-term land productivity. These can include careful nutrient management, maintaining drainage systems, targeted erosion control, grass waterways, buffer strips, rotational grazing, crop rotation, cover cropping, or establishing wildlife and pollinator habitats. None of these practices are new — they're proven, adaptable strategies farmers have successfully integrated into operations for generations.

You don't have to drastically change your farming style to see benefits. Even modest adjustments tailored to your farm's unique situation can lead to more consistent yields and ROI, improved soil health, and a greater sense of pride in how your land is managed.

6. Connect with the Next Generation of Farmers

Many landowners are finding new ways to ensure their farms remain productive and well cared for by forming partnerships with young or beginning farmers. These relationships can take many forms — long-term leases, mentorships, or gradual ownership transitions — and they don't have to be high-risk. In fact, when structured thoughtfully, they can provide dependable income for your family while offering a motivated steward a rare chance to farm.

Organizations like American Farmland Trust and FarmAdvisors.ag can help connect you with well-prepared beginning farmers and offer resources to reduce risk and ensure alignment of goals.

7. *Work with Advisors Who Understand Your Values*

A trusted farmland advisor, farm management specialist, or estate planning professional can help you create a practical plan — whether through leases, sales, succession planning, or estate strategies — that aligns clearly with your family's values and personal objectives. You don't have to navigate these important decisions alone. Thoughtful guidance ensures your vision for the land and your family becomes reality. If considering complex solutions like conservation easements or deed restrictions, it's important to never make these critical decisions alone. Expert advice from qualified professionals, including attorneys, financial advisors, and land specialists, is essential to navigating the detailed legal, financial, and stewardship implications involved.

CHOOSING YOUR BEST PATH FORWARD

Throughout this chapter, we've explored how your farmland decisions touch your neighbors, your community, and generations to come. You've seen how thoughtful decisions about your farmland can help protect rural communities, support local economies, and preserve a way of life worth passing forward. Whether you're actively farming, leasing your land, or preparing to transition ownership, stewardship doesn't end when your name leaves the deed. In fact, your most meaningful impact can begin precisely at the moment you decide how to move forward.

Whether you decide to keep, sell, or reimagine your farm, your decisions will shape your community's future just as much as your family's. By thoughtfully considering how you pass along your farm, you ensure your land continues thriving, serving, and contributing long after you've stepped back from daily management.

Now that you have clarity on the importance of stewardship and legacy, you're ready for the next practical steps.

In Chapter 8, you'll see how families like yours have successfully navigated challenges, discovered creative solutions, and kept their farms productive, meaningful, and aligned with their life goals.

> Whether you're actively farming, leasing your land, or preparing to transition ownership, stewardship doesn't end when your name leaves the deed.

In Chapter 9, we'll explore how other families thoughtfully chose to sell, turning what might feel like an ending into a meaningful new chapter that protects family relationships, community values, and personal goals.

CLEAR CHOICES, LASTING LEGACY:

Stewardship Decisions for Your Family Farm

CHAPTER 8

Strategic Solutions for Keeping the Farm

As Emily and her family talked some more during the Christmas holiday, she confronted the fact that she'd reached a breaking point in her career. Years of working in corporate agriculture had taken their toll, leaving her drained, disconnected, and longing for something deeper. As she stood in the living room, scanning the fields through the back door, she finally said aloud what she'd been holding inside for so long.

"I don't want to miss another one of Brayden and Olivia's milestones," she confessed. "This farm isn't just land to me. It's our chance to build something real and rooted in our family's values. I want our kids to feel connected to this place, our history, and our family."

Jake, sitting on the couch with Brandon watching a football game, nodded. "I've always seen this farm as something bigger," he admitted. "Success doesn't have to be about a paycheck; it can be about living our purpose, together."

Brandon had initially been skeptical about doing anything new with the farm. However, after several conversations with Emily, he realized that the future they all wanted didn't have to depend on expanding their acreage. Instead of chasing more land or taking on more debt, they could focus on using what they had more intentionally.

"I agree that we don't need more acres," Brandon added. "I think we can use what we have more creatively. We can build on the practices we've already started, like growing our relay crops and expanding our rotational grazing. If we land that alfalfa contract with the local dairy, we could increase profits without adding acres or risk."

Energized by where the conversation was heading, Emily sat in a chair across from them. "So, the wedding venue is on?"

Brandon grinned. "I'm in. But we'll have to convince Grandpa Jim to get on board."

Of course, growth makes sense for some families. But for the Taylors, deepening their connection to the land and diversifying income streams on their existing acreage felt more aligned with their values and capacity.

The Taylors knew from the start that their plan wouldn't be easy. And, like most families who make bold choices, they soon discovered that dreaming big and making those dreams a reality were two different things.

Fueled by her excitement, Emily stepped away from her corporate job to lead the barn renovation, pouring her energy into transforming a space that had stood unchanged for generations. Brandon dove deeper into regenerative agriculture practices, exploring new markets and partnerships. Jake continued his daily commute, balancing family responsibilities with financial stability. Yet, inevitably, optimism collided with reality. Construction delays, unexpected repairs, mounting expenses, and the stress that accompanies meaningful change all started to pile up.

One afternoon, Emily stood in the half-renovated barn staring at exposed beams and a shrinking budget. Jake arrived home, weary from another long day, just in time for frustration to spill over.

"Everything is falling apart," Emily said, her voice strained with tension. "The foundation is worse than we expected, our timeline is blown, and Brandon's stressed about cash flow. I feel like I'm doing all of this alone. Do you even want this to succeed?"

Jake's frustration flashed. "Are you kidding? I'm working overtime to keep us stable financially, and now you're questioning my commitment?"

Their exchange hung heavily in the air. Brandon, hearing raised voices from across the yard, approached quietly. "I get the stress," he said calmly, looking at both of them. "But budgets matter. I've spent years protecting this farm from financial ruin. We can't forget that."

Emily's voice softened. "Brandon, I know this feels risky, but it's not some reckless idea. This is our future."

That night, Grandpa Jim sat with Emily by the farmhouse pond, the evening stillness surrounding them. "When your grandmother and I took over this farm, we had setbacks, too. Change is always harder than we expect, but it's worth it," he said gently.

He paused for a moment before continuing, "Remember, you all have different strengths. Jake understands the financial side. Brandon knows the land. And you? You have vision. When things get tough, you need each other even more."

Jim's words sparked something powerful in Emily. Sure, they needed clarity. But they needed unity even more. So, Emily called a family meeting — one focused not on problems, but on possibilities.

As they gathered around the kitchen table again, Emily took a deep breath. "I'm sorry for getting overwhelmed," she said sincerely. "Jake, your financial caution matters. Brandon, your commitment to protecting the farm matters. I can't do this alone."

Jake nodded. "We can revisit our budget, find breathing room, and make adjustments."

Brandon's shoulders dropped as he let out a deep sigh. "And if we stay aligned on the big picture, I can handle a little uncertainty."

That conversation didn't erase every difficulty, but it built their resilience. By openly acknowledging their challenges, clarifying their shared purpose, and leaning into each person's unique strengths, the Taylors transformed the tension into teamwork.

COMMON REASONS TO KEEP A FARM

Recognizing that you're not the first family to wrestle with the decision to keep or sell inherited farmland should bring you an immense amount of peace. It means that you can look at what others have done as a model of what might work for your family. Maybe your family is facing a crossroads, much like the Taylors. Perhaps you're wondering if you can realistically keep your farm in a way that aligns with your family's personal goals, financial needs, and emotional well-being.

The short answer is yes, but it requires intentionality, creativity, and clear-eyed strategic thinking.

In my experience supporting my clients through this process, I've found there are three primary reasons people choose to keep their farm: for financial security and wealth-building, to preserve a legacy and stewardship, or because of the lifestyle and identity associated with land ownership.

Financial Security and Wealth-Building

For heirs not actively farming, leasing to a family member or tenant can generate consistent rental income, providing steady support with relatively low effort. For the farming heir, continued access to the land is vital. Owning rather than renting protects long-term operational security and investment in equipment, livestock, or land improvements. And, because farmland has historically appreciated in value, whether you're operating it or holding it as an investment, it can serve as a cornerstone of multi-generational wealth.

Keeping the farm can open up several smart financial strategies to protect its value over time. Depending on your goals, these might include stepped-up basis benefits, long-term depreciation, family partnerships, or a 1031 exchange. These tools aren't reserved for large operations — they're often most impactful for families like yours who want time, flexibility, and options.

You don't need to have all the answers right now, and you don't have to do it alone. Trusted advisors, CPAs, or estate planners can walk you through what's most useful for your specific situation.

Legacy and Stewardship

Farming families often feel the weight of generations who came before them, and the land often includes barns, woods, fields, and waterways with emotional significance. Keeping the farm is a way of acknowledging the sacrifices made by previous generations and continuing to share the physical reminders of countless memories.

For the person actively farming, the land is often closely tied to their identity, pride, and desire to preserve their family's heritage. Keeping the farm affirms that identity and supports their ongoing commitment to the land. Additionally, keeping the farm provides an on-ramp for the next generation to enter agriculture through mentorship, lease-to-own agreements, or gradual involvement or ownership in the operation. Holding onto the farm prevents unwanted development or sale to outside entities. It allows families to align land use with conservation, community, and sound farming practices.

Lifestyle, Identity, and Well-Being

For many farmers, the land is their job site *and* their home. Keeping it helps maintain a core part of their identity, livelihood, and self-worth. It allows for a lifestyle that's grounded in purpose, proximity to family, and the rhythms of the seasons. It's a central place to visit for reunions, holidays, hunting season, or to simply feel a deep sense of belonging.

Because of this, keeping the land can serve as a rallying point, especially if the family develops a shared vision for stewardship, investment, or future transition. Retaining ownership also creates space to shift strategies, diversify income (through agritourism, direct-to-consumer sales, or conservation programs), and innovate.

PUTTING YOUR STRENGTHS TO WORK

The Taylors had a breakthrough when they shifted from focusing on problems to leveraging each family member's strengths. Once the tension broke and the conversations got real, the Taylors did what resilient families do best: they got to work — together. But this time, they embraced each other's unique strengths.

Jake started a fresh spreadsheet that included milestones tied to their goals and Emily's vision. It accounted for what they needed to *feel* stable, not just stay solvent. Emily revisited the renovation plans, this time prioritizing the essentials. She mapped out a realistic timeline and scaled back a lot of extras that didn't serve their long-term goals. Brandon stepped in with quiet resolve. "Tell me what you need," he said. Everyone had a lane. Everyone had a role.

And then there was Lisa, their mother. She hadn't spoken much during early planning, but when the first inquiries about the venue came in, she stepped forward. With a background in customer service at diners, office lobbies, and through her volunteer work, Lisa became the heartbeat of hospitality. She handled bookings, welcomed guests, and coordinated vendors. Her joy was contagious. Watching brides light up? Watching guests linger by the pond? Those moments were precious to her. Caring for their guests was her second act and gave her a renewed sense of purpose and pride.

Brandon thrived, too. He expanded his regenerative practices, partnered with a local dairy for hay contracts, and launched a direct-to-consumer beef program. Jake discovered that spreadsheets can be deeply fulfilling when they help build something meaningful. He took over the business side of their new venture and managed cash flow planning, vendor relationships, and creative partnerships with local businesses.

And Emily? She wasn't just the visionary anymore. She was the thread that wove it all together. She preserved the old wooden beams in the barn and added just the right touches of modernity with wildflowers, lanterns, and warmth.

The first wedding wasn't flawless, but it was full of heart. A caterer arrived late, the sound system glitched, and they had to improvise when a rainstorm rolled through. But guests laughed, lingered by the pond, and created memories that felt timeless. Grandpa Jim watched it all. One day, he whispered to Emily, "I wasn't sure at first, but you've brought life back to this place and given this place a heartbeat again."

Not every idea works out perfectly. And not every family has the time or capital to start a new venture. The Taylors' story is one example of what's possible when teamwork, creativity, and shared values align. Your solution might look different, and that's more than okay.

The Taylors were living their values *on their terms*. They succeeded because they leaned into the strengths of each family member and matched those strengths to clear, shared goals.

The Taylors' solution focused on regenerative and creative strategies, but it's important to remember that conventional agricultural practices also play a crucial role in feeding communities and maintaining rural economies. Both conventional and regenerative practices, when implemented thoughtfully, can enhance farm profitability, sustainability, and long-term viability. Your family's approach should reflect what's practical, achievable, and aligned with your values.

DISCOVER YOUR FAMILY'S HIDDEN STRENGTHS

Like the Taylors, your family has unique talents, resources, and passions waiting to be unlocked. And while a wedding venue might not be the solution for you, simply start by identifying clearly what each person already brings to the table. Phase 5 of the LAND VALUES framework is all about strategy and building a plan that reflects everyone's strengths and goals.

If you're planning to keep your farm and you need to develop creative solutions for reimagining the farm's operations, here's how to start identifying your family's hidden strengths:

1. **Make a simple list**. Write down each family member's name (including those not currently farming).
2. **Identify each person's natural strengths**. Consider their professional skills, life experiences, personal qualities, and emotional roles (for example, strategic thinking, creativity, organizational skills, relationship-building).

3. **Explore untapped passions or interests**. Often, the best ideas for reimagining your farm come from unexpected places, such as a family member's hospitality skills, marketing know-how, financial expertise, or commitment to conservation.

4. **Discuss openly**. Create a supportive, judgment-free space to talk about how each person's strengths might contribute positively to the farm's future.

When each family member's abilities are recognized and leveraged intentionally, you create a pathway forward that's grounded in your real-life values, goals, and possibilities.

DESIGNING A FARM THAT SERVES YOUR FAMILY'S GOALS

After the Taylors clarified their family's strengths, they didn't rush straight into detailed budgets or logistics. Instead, they paused and asked one critical Return on Life question: "If everything goes right, what does our ideal life look like five years from now, and how does the farm help us get there?"

This simple but powerful question changed their entire approach. Instead of reacting to immediate pressures, they were designing their path based on their core values and long-term aspirations. The clearer their vision became, the easier it became to make strategic decisions about budgets, renovations, new income streams, and community engagement.

Together, they began to articulate a vivid, shared picture of success. Emily envisioned hosting memorable gatherings in the barn, reconnecting with the community, and supporting the family financially. Jake saw a farm that supported their financial security, balanced work with family time, and aligned with his personal desire for meaningful work. Brandon imagined a thriving regenerative agriculture system that drew recognition, income, and pride without the pressure of continuous expansion. And Lisa pictured herself welcoming visitors, building connections, and finally having a meaningful role she genuinely loved. As a result, their farm became not just productive land, but a place aligned perfectly with their family's lives, values, and dreams.

As you consider your farm's future and create your own vision, gather your family and create an open, relaxed environment. Give everyone a chance to speak without interruption or judgment. Invite each person to describe their ideal scenario for the farm five or ten years from now. Encourage them to think deeply about lifestyle, relationships, financial stability, community involvement, and emotional well-being.

Actively listen and look for patterns, shared goals, and opportunities that emerge. Then, combine the ideas into a shared vision statement, capturing the core purpose, values, and concrete goals your family truly agrees upon.

Here are a few examples of what your family's vision might be:

- Our farm operates as a profitable, resilient enterprise that secures our family's financial future while enhancing our overall quality of life. Through strategic management, thoughtful stewardship, and diversified income streams, it generates sustainable profit and cash flow, supports meaningful family engagement, and serves as a foundation for long-term generational wealth. Our goal is to ensure that each generation finds personal fulfillment, stability, and opportunity in connection to the land.
- Our farm is a thriving center for regenerative agriculture and community engagement. It's a place that supports our financial stability, brings our family closer

together, and strengthens our connection to the land and local community.

- Our farm continues to be a sustainable and profitable agricultural business, managed efficiently with modern practices that support steady income and long-term stability. It offers rewarding work, clear decision-making processes, and practical opportunities for the next generation to learn and participate actively in its operation.

Once you have this clear vision, strategy becomes much simpler. Budgets, business plans, and timelines align naturally with your family's deeper purpose.

Next, we'll explore specific creative strategies and practical examples that other farm families have successfully used to keep their farms viable and meaningful, so you can see how your vision could translate into real-world solutions.

CREATIVE STRATEGIES FOR KEEPING YOUR FARM

Once your family clearly understands the type of future you want your farm to support, the next step is translating that vision into practical, achievable strategies. Remember, there's no one-size-fits-all approach. Your solution should fit your family's unique strengths, circumstances, and goals.

The Taylors' solution was to reimagine parts of their farm to include a wedding venue, a direct-to-consumer beef program, and a family-run event space. Your solution might look very different. The point isn't the model. It's the mindset. The Taylors succeeded because they didn't just ask, "Can we afford to keep the farm?" Instead, they adopted a Return on Life mindset and asked, "What kind of life do we want this farm to support?"

And what made their success sustainable? Their values. They didn't chase expansion; they deepened their impact. They didn't divide duties; they unified purpose. They didn't just preserve; they evolved.

For your family, a creative Return on Life strategy might look like:

- Embracing expansion as the key to success
- Partnering with a young farmer
- Adding a direct-to-consumer business model
- Implementing a farm stay/weekend getaway program
- Working with local schools or community groups
- Exploring agricultural easements and legacy trusts
- Hosting agritourism weekends or educational events
- Selective timber harvests, hunting leases, or alternative markets

Each of these strategies is rooted in the idea of aligning your farming practices directly with your family's vision and life goals. By starting with your vision, you ensure your decisions aren't driven by pressure or short-term financial fears, but by your genuine desires for a meaningful, profitable, and sustainable farm. Some of these ideas may not apply to your situation, and that's okay. The goal is to create a plan that reflects your family's values and strengths. If it supports your values, your people, and your purpose, then it's Return on Life strategy at its best.

As you consider these strategies, reflect on these questions with your family:

- Which of these options aligns most closely with our family's vision, resources, and values?
- What steps can we realistically take right now to explore these possibilities?

- How might these approaches increase both our farm's profitability and our personal fulfillment?

When considering stewardship strategies like conservation easements, deed restrictions, or long-term leases, ask these key questions to ensure your decisions are well-informed:

- Are we comfortable with permanent restrictions on future land use and development options?
- Do we fully understand any required financial commitments, such as stewardship endowments, monitoring fees, or other ongoing costs?
- Have we considered how these stewardship decisions might affect our land's future market value and our ability to sell or transfer it later?
- Have we sought professional advice from qualified conservation attorneys, financial advisors, and estate planning specialists who understand farmland-specific issues?

By asking and answering these questions openly, you'll uncover a path forward that feels clear, confident, purposeful, and reflective of your family's values and aspirations.

IS KEEPING THE FARM A VIABLE OPTION?

By now, you might be thinking, This sounds inspiring, but can we realistically keep our farm? Is this actually doable for us?

You're wise to ask these questions clearly and directly. Keeping your farm is about making strategic decisions that genuinely align with your family's life goals and practical realities. To do this, you need to consider four key areas:

1. Financial viability
2. Emotional viability
3. Personal and family viability
4. Community and legacy viability

I've provided a list of questions for you to answer to gain clarity around each of these categories and uncover whether keeping your farm is the right option for you. Remember to think about your responses through a Return on Life mindset and keep your most important land values in mind. If you need a refresher on either of these topics, you can return to Chapters 3 and 4.

Financial Viability

To determine whether keeping your farmland is a financially viable option, start by asking these objective, clear-eyed financial questions:

- What is our current income from the farm, and can it sustainably meet our needs long-term?
- Are there realistic ways to diversify income (e.g., implementing regenerative practices, niche markets, strategic alternatives) or reduce expenses?
- Would new enterprises or revenue streams (like agritourism or direct-to-consumer sales) significantly improve profitability?
- Does growing the operation in size create the viability we need or desire? Or does the risk outweigh the reward?

If financial stress is your biggest obstacle, your solution might be diversifying your farm's income, shifting operational practices, or adjusting your business model creatively rather than expanding or taking on new debt.

Emotional Viability

Emotional sustainability matters just as much as financial stability, and your farm should support your emotional well-being and enhance your life. To determine the emotional impact that keeping your farm has on your life, answer the following questions:

- Does holding onto the farm enhance our quality of life, or does it add emotional strain or stress?
- Are we holding on out of genuine desire or out of obligation, guilt, or fear of change?
- Could creative changes to our operations or roles within the farm improve our emotional satisfaction and reduce stress?

It's unrealistic to believe that owning and stewarding farmland will always be a completely stress-free experience, but there are many ways to operate a farm that increase your quality of life.

Personal and Family Viability

Keeping your farm must clearly align with your family's personal goals and strengths. Answer these questions to get a better understanding of the people who might be impacted by your decision to keep the farm:

- Do my family members have the interest, skills, and commitment to actively contribute to farm management?
- Could roles and responsibilities be adjusted creatively to better match each person's abilities and interests?
- How would keeping the farm serve our long-term family relationships, unity, and shared vision for the future?

If your family's talents and interests align naturally with the farm, you've got a powerful foundation for success. If they don't, carefully consider if adjustments can be realistically made or if alternative paths might serve everyone better.

Community and Legacy Viability

Finally, like we talked about in Chapter 7, consider how your farm supports your local community:

- Does our farm currently benefit our community in ways we value?
- Are there opportunities to deepen community ties through agritourism, direct sales, or conservation initiatives?
- Would continuing our farm align meaningfully with the family traditions we want to pass on to future generations and our community?

Reflecting on your farm's generational and community impact can help you see its deeper value and allow you to identify how it aligns with your personal goals and values.

If all of this information feels like a lot to consider right now, review the LAND VALUES framework and take things one step at a time. Here are the five phases of the framework at a glance:

1. **Listen:** Understand each other's perspectives.
2. **Acknowledge:** Validate each family member's emotional connections.
3. **Name Priorities:** Clearly define the values guiding your family's choices
4. **Define Scenarios:** Identify practical options for the farm's future.
5. **Strategize:** Move forward with a unified, actionable plan.

RECOGNIZING YOUR TRUE WEALTH

The Taylors succeeded because they got honest about their needs, clear about their values, and creative in aligning their farm's future with their family's goals. They realized their farm's wealth was found in the land *and* in their ability to work together by using each person's unique strengths and passions to shape a life that felt purposeful and fulfilling.

Throughout this chapter, you've also begun that crucial journey of reflection, evaluation, and practical planning. You've asked important questions that will allow you to actively design a meaningful future built on clarity, confidence, and shared purpose, and you've aligned the way you manage your land with the life you want to build. This is what Return on Life looks like in practice.

Keeping your farm should feel intentional and empowering, not driven by guilt, pressure, or fear of change. For some families, it brings deep meaning and purpose. For others, a different path forward better honors their season of life. What matters most is that your decision reflects your family's values.

The LAND VALUES framework helped the Taylors match their individual strengths with a shared plan that allowed them to turn their vision into something real. The result? A farm that reflected not just their history, but also their hopes for the future. Ultimately, the legacy you leave is measured in more than land. It's measured by how your decisions reflect your family's core values, enrich your lives, and strengthen the bonds that truly matter.

As a reminder, conservation easements, stewardship agreements, and other land-use restrictions involve complex and often permanent commitments that can significantly impact your family's flexibility, future property value, and financial plans. Always engage with qualified professionals, including

The legacy you leave is
measured in more than land.
It's measured by how your
decisions reflect your
family's core values,
enrich your lives,
and strengthen
the bonds that
truly matter.

———————————————

attorneys, financial advisors, and land specialists who fully understand the complexities involved, to ensure your decisions align clearly with your family's long-term goals and values.

Download The Return on Life Mindset Reflection Worksheet and Chapter Summary

Visit AmericanFamilyFarmlands.com/downloads to download a no-cost, one-page worksheet that captures key takeaways, outlines the Return on Life mindset you need to succeed, and summarizes critical action steps in the LAND VALUES framework.

CHAPTER 9

When Selling Is the Best Option

The air felt heavy with heat and impending storms. The mood hung equally heavy around Pat's kitchen table. The financials had come through, and it was clear there was no easy path toward keeping the farm. There were too many considerations to contend with, and although each member of the family had been trying to find a workable solution for months, no sibling had the money to buy the others out.

Silence filled the room; each person was hesitant to voice the truth they'd been quietly struggling with. Finally, Linda whispered, "I can't help but feel we're letting Mom and Dad down if we sell. This farm was their dream." Her words mirrored what everyone else felt but hadn't yet said aloud.

Pat nodded slowly and said, "I feel the same way, Linda. But there are nine of us spread across the country, each with different needs and dreams. I keep wondering if we're really struggling to preserve the farm, or something else we can't quite name."

Then Mike spoke up, his voice gentle, but firm. "If we don't figure this out soon, the decision only gets harder. Nine owners today could easily become twenty tomorrow. Imagine trying to reach an agreement then. Is that really the kind of legacy Mom and Dad would have wanted us to pass down?"

The others shifted a little in their seats. Mike had named the real fear: that holding onto the farm out of obligation might actually mean passing along confusion, complexity, and tension rather than clarity and strength.

In the quiet that followed, Pat offered a perspective he'd come to believe was the best option after thinking about the situation with a Return on Life mindset and working through the LAND VALUES framework. "Maybe selling isn't about giving up the legacy our parents built," he said. "Maybe it's about carrying on their values and memories in a way that honors who we are now, rather than who we used to be."

In that moment, the tension in the room started to disappear as everyone began to accept that this decision was about freedom, clarity, and respect for their parents' sacrifices and for their own futures. Selling the farm didn't have to be a mark of failure. It could be an equally viable show of courage.

"I realize I'm holding onto the farm because it's tied to who I am," Pat said. "But I also feel that keeping it isn't the only way to honor our parents. And I'd be all right with selling it as long as it could go to someone who will carry on the same values we have."

Linda's shoulders relaxed. "Oh, I'm so glad to hear that. I didn't know how to tell you I felt overwhelmed. I thought it made me selfish to say so."

Mike gave a small smile of relief. "Honestly, I've felt stuck for years. The farm is special, but I think it's just as important that our family can finally move forward and do other things we've wanted to do."

Roger looked around the table. "You all know I've wanted to just sell the place, but that's because it'll be so hard to let it go." He sighed. "And yet, I also know keeping it isn't going to bring Mom and Dad back. The farm is a burden we don't need." He swallowed. "I know we'll find the right buyer — someone who'll treat the place right, maybe fix it up more too — and we'll get a good price. Let's start figuring all of that out so we can make Mom and Dad proud."

Sometimes, despite careful thought and best intentions, the most honest and courageous choice is letting go. Whether you're an heir, executor, a trustee, or the person who's farmed the land for 40 years, if selling gives you peace, security, and forward momentum, it may be the wisest choice you can make.

Still, knowing it's the right decision doesn't necessarily make it easy. It's hard to let go of the place that is the heart of family memories, the keeper of traditions, and the symbol of generational sacrifices. However, selling inherited farmland can mean choosing to honor your family's heritage in ways that genuinely reflect who you and your family have become.

> Selling inherited farmland can mean choosing to honor your family's heritage in ways that genuinely reflect who you and your family have become.

COMMON REASONS TO SELL YOUR FARM

Families who retain their land often do so because they recognize its value as a source of stability, history, and opportunity for future generations. And yet, if these things come at a cost you don't feel you can pay, you may need to find different ways to express your values.

For some families, selling offers clarity, closure, and a chance to reinvest in current goals, especially when holding on leads to ongoing strain or difficult compromises. For others, working through the complexities to retain the land is worth the effort because it honors shared purpose or long-term dreams. The best solution for you is the one that brings peace, alignment, and possibility.

Here are some of the most common reasons families choose to sell their farm:

Complex Inheritance and Family Dynamics

When multiple heirs inherit the farm — especially across generations or geographic distances — decision-making becomes hard. For heirs who live far away or who no longer have ties to the land, keeping the farm may not feel relevant. Selling the farm can offer a clean resolution, allow for reinvestment in current goals, and help preserve relationships that might otherwise fracture under ongoing disagreement.

For the sibling or family member actively farming, the pressure of representing the entire family's history on the land while managing daily operations can be overwhelming. When consensus can't be reached, selling may offer emotional and financial relief. Similarly, if one family member farmed the land for years while others contributed little, selling can be a way to level the playing field when no internal buyout or restructuring agreement is feasible.

The Farm Has Become a Burden

If no one steps up to lead or manage the asset, the farm can deteriorate quickly. Selling may become the best way to preserve its value before it declines further. Leasing is always an option, but for heirs not farming, leasing income may be minimal once split among multiple stakeholders. Add in taxes, insurance, and upkeep, and the land may be costing more than it provides. Situations like this can be further complicated if the lease is held by a family member and they're paying below market rate. In this case, other heirs may resent this imbalance and view selling as a way to regain financial alignment.

For the actively farming family member, trying to carry both the business and the family's emotional expectations can lead to burnout. Selling (or partially selling) can create breathing room or allow them to reinvest in more manageable operations.

Selling Unlocks Opportunity

Depending on your timing and goals, a sale may also offer tax-smart options. These can include capital gains planning, stepped-up basis benefits, reinvestment through a 1031 exchange, or even charitable giving strategies. These approaches aren't just for large estates. Many families use them to align the sale with personal goals or community impact. You don't have to figure it all out alone. Working with a trusted advisor, accountant, or attorney can help you evaluate what fits your situation best.

A clean sale can help prevent estate disputes, probate delays, or unclear title issues that might create long-term stress or liability. It also allows everyone to receive a portion of the inheritance and use the funds in ways that best align with their personal goals, such as paying off debt, investing, starting a business, or funding education. And even for the person actively farming, a sale can open new doors to transition to a smaller operation, reinvest in other land, or step into a new season of life.

Market Timing and Strong Returns

When market conditions are strong, selling may be the most financially responsible move. Competitive bidding, investor interest, and limited inventory can drive prices well above expectations. In areas facing development, zoning shifts, or uncertain ag economics, selling while prices are high may secure long-term financial stability, especially for those near retirement or looking to simplify their life.

Sometimes, the farming heir recognizes that the financial and emotional returns just don't justify continuing. Selling at the right time can protect their future and allow them to pivot with purpose. More often than not, preparing is more than just getting organized; it's helping everyone move forward, no matter the decision or outcome.

The Farm No Longer Aligns with Family Values or Lifestyle

Urban careers, changing life goals, and personal transformations often mean that the daily operations of farming no longer align with what the family values most. For many, the complexity of managing leases, disputes, tax issues, and emotional obligations becomes too much. If none of the heirs plan to farm and the farming family member is ready to move on, selling may feel like a natural, peaceful next step.

STRATEGIC PREPARATION FOR A MEANINGFUL SALE

Pat's family knew selling the farm to the right buyer for the right price would take more than pounding a "For Sale" sign into the front yard. Back at their kitchen table for another meeting, I said, "Now that you've decided to sell, you need to understand your Foundation of Value. These are the pieces that give buyers confidence, tell your farm's story, and maximize returns."

Their first step was to gather and clearly document the farm's history, performance, and value. Buyers today are looking at more than just the soil and fence lines — they're looking for proof of productivity, returns, stewardship, care, and opportunity. So, instead of just listing acreage, Pat's family created a compelling narrative around the land's story, including:

- Detailed soil fertility and productivity reports to clearly demonstrate yield history and management practices.
- Clear documentation of infrastructure and improvements, including drainage, tiling, fencing, and buildings, to show potential buyers the tangible investments made in the farm.
- Timber analysis that fully evaluated the timber resources, volume, species, quality, and potential market value.
- Lease agreements and tenant history that documented the quality of stewardship from Pat's father's era to the current farm tenant, providing full transparency around existing agreements.

Initially, some of Pat's family members believed gathering paperwork and assessing the farm's value would only be necessary if they chose to sell. As they moved through the LAND VALUES framework and began gathering records, clarifying ownership, and understanding the market, something unexpected happened. Yes, they felt more prepared. But they also felt something else: peace. The burden of not knowing lifted. The pressure of disagreement eased. And the family began to talk again — not just about price, but about purpose, regardless of whether they decided to sell, keep, or transition their farm.

During one family meeting to review documents, Linda noted, "Wow! Even if we waited five more years to sell or chose not to sell at all, this process has already been worth it. Now we really understand what we have, and we're ready to make a confident decision when the time comes."

Pat nodded, smiling. "We're not guessing anymore. I don't know about the rest of you, but clearly knowing where we stand has brought more peace than I've felt in quite some time."

By thoughtfully documenting their farm's productivity, infrastructure, stewardship, and legal ownership details, they discovered they'd created the clarity they so desperately needed. Instead of worrying, debating, or guessing about their options, they could now confidently discuss plans and opportunities based on clear, reliable information.

Their preparation also gave them the opportunity to improve their current management decisions. Because they now had clear documentation about yields, soil fertility, conservation practices, and lease structures, they found themselves empowered to make stronger, smarter stewardship choices that enhanced their farm's value no matter what they ultimately decided.

In other words, the simple act of thoughtful preparation provided lasting benefits beyond a potential sale:

- It gave them financial clarity, helping them confidently plan retirement, estate decisions, and family financial goals.
- It created emotional relief and stronger family communication, reducing misunderstandings and aligning everyone around clear, shared facts.

- It allowed them to proactively strengthen their lease agreements and tenant relationships, protecting both their farm's productivity and their long-term value.
- It provided them with the flexibility to act quickly and confidently, whether market conditions changed, family needs evolved, or new opportunities arose.

"I thought preparing these documents was just a step we needed to complete if we were committed to selling," Mike said, leaning back in his chair with a sigh of relief as he finished looking at the numbers. "Now I see it's really about giving us freedom, no matter what happens next."

Next, we focused on clearly defining their ownership structure and resolving any title or legal uncertainties. Clarifying the farm's tenants-in-common structure and proactively addressing probate or title concerns prevented future complications and helped maintain family harmony throughout the sales process.

We also strategically planned the timing of their sale, carefully evaluating local market conditions, farmland and timber values, and buyer interest. Pat's family learned firsthand that an effective sales approach includes a strategic listing price and precisely timed market entry, aligning clearly with buyer demand and optimal market conditions. By proactively addressing documentation, ownership clarity, and strategic market timing, the family felt increasingly confident, empowered, and at peace with their decision to sell. In fact, Pat called me one morning and said, "I never realized how powerful preparation could be. I feel proud knowing we're selling this farm responsibly."

KNOW YOUR FARM'S TRUE MARKET VALUE

One of the most common pitfalls I see families face when considering selling their farm is relying on guesswork, anecdotes, or neighbors' stories rather than clear, reliable data. However, taking thoughtful steps to gather the necessary documents and reports to understand the true value of your farmland doesn't commit you to a sale. As Pat and his family discovered, it empowers you to clearly understand exactly what you have, what options are genuinely available, and how your land can support your family's goals. Preparation, in the truest sense, is about stewardship and ensuring your family remains empowered, flexible, and confident no matter what path you choose next.

> Preparation, in the truest sense, is about stewardship and ensuring your family remains empowered, flexible, and confident no matter what path you choose next.

With Pat's family, early conversations were dominated by vague comparisons and assumptions, like, "The neighbor's farm sold last year for an impressive price. Ours must be worth more because we've always had better soil." Or "My friend said farmland values are dropping. We need to get this sold now."

These stories and the coffeeshop talk, while compelling, rarely lead to clear-headed decisions. Instead, they often create confusion, unrealistic expectations, and unnecessary anxiety. To avoid this, Pat's family chose to obtain a professional farmland appraisal, updated timber valuation, and clear market analysis. "We don't want to guess. We want to *know*," Pat said. "Every family member needs more than just the coffeeshop talk."

To ensure Pat's family had all the data they needed, we carefully walked through three straightforward steps to ensure the family had an accurate understanding of their farm's Foundation of Value.

Step 1: Professional Farmland and Timber Appraisal

We brought in a certified farmland appraiser who understood local soils, productivity, and recent comparable sales. We hired a certified forester to walk the wooded acreage and determine the market value. These appraisals became the cornerstone of their entire decision-making process, providing a clear, realistic value that everyone trusted.

Step 2: Local Market Analysis

Building on the certified appraisal, we took a deeper dive into recent local farmland sales to better understand what motivated buyers in terms of final prices and the broader opportunities driving market value. We closely evaluated factors like proximity to grain elevators and major transportation routes, availability and quality of drainage infrastructure, and potential for alternative land uses, impact opportunities, and conservation initiatives valued by the local community. By identifying these tangible community benefits beyond mere acreage, we uncovered additional opportunities that significantly informed our strategic decisions.

Step 3: Strategic Pricing Decisions

Armed with accurate market and timber information, Pat's family was able to set clear, realistic expectations. They didn't price the farm too high out of emotional attachment or too low out of anxiety. Instead, they priced strategically and fairly in a way that aligned with what serious local buyers would confidently pay.

"Once we had the data, including the timber value, we weren't guessing anymore," Pat told me. "Suddenly, we were having productive conversations, not emotional ones. It changed everything."

Real preparation creates the freedom to make the right one.

HOW KNOWING YOUR FARM'S VALUE HELPS YOU

Understanding your farm's real market value will ensure a good selling price and empower your family to make informed, confident decisions. Clear market valuation provides you with:

- **Realistic expectations** so you can reduce frustration by aligning your family's hopes with what buyers actually value.
- **Stronger negotiations** so you can confidently and fairly negotiate offers, avoiding emotional reactions or unnecessary compromises.
- **Reduced family stress** by replacing guesswork and vague stories with reliable, transparent data everyone can understand and trust.
- **Flexibility to act** because clearly knowing your farm's true value means you're ready and empowered to act decisively, whether you choose to sell soon, later, or hold the land for generations.

If your family is still unsure about your farm's value, ask yourselves honestly:

- Have we had a professional appraisal within the last year or two?
- Do we genuinely understand local market conditions?
- Are our price expectations based on verifiable data rather than emotional guesses?
- Could clarity from a local expert on market value reduce family tension and help us make better decisions?

WHEN SELLING IS THE BEST OPTION

Just as it did for Pat's family, obtaining a clear, professional appraisal and market analysis gives your family confidence, unity, and peace of mind, no matter what decisions lie ahead.

CLARIFYING YOUR OWNERSHIP STRUCTURE AND TITLE

It's hard to talk about title paperwork or ownership structures when your heart is wrapped up in the land. But clarity here isn't just about legality — it's about reducing stress, protecting relationships, and keeping decision-making fair and forward-focused.

When families reach the point of seriously considering selling their farmland, it's common to encounter unexpected complications around ownership structure and property titles. Often, these issues only emerge late in the process, leading to delays, frustration, and even family conflict.

Pat's family knew they wanted to avoid these challenges, so early in our conversations, Pat brought up a critical concern. He said, "We inherited this farm as joint tenants, which means the major decisions require unanimous agreement. How will we navigate this when we sell?"

Pat wasn't alone. Many families inherit property under similar circumstances. And while allowing siblings, spouses, and cousins to hold some form of ownership can seem straightforward initially, it often becomes a source of tension and confusion later.

Clarifying your ownership structure and confirming a clean property title is a vital part of ensuring your family's harmony and protecting your financial legacy. When ownership isn't clear, simple decisions become complicated, disagreements become more common, transactions get delayed, relationships can become strained, and financial outcomes suffer. By addressing ownership clarity early, your family can approach selling your farm with confidence, unity, and peace of mind.

A Simple Approach to Understanding Ownership

Pat's family followed straightforward steps to ensure their property ownership was easy to understand and manage:

1. **Confirm Ownership Structure.** Pat and his siblings carefully reviewed their current ownership arrangement to understand how it would affect their decisions and financial outcomes. This discussion helped reveal opportunities and opened doors to clearer choices.
2. **Conduct a Title Review.** They performed a detailed review of the property title, checking for any liens, unresolved estate issues, or outdated documents. Addressing these items proactively helped avoid unexpected complications down the road.
3. **Evaluate and Simplify.** With professional legal guidance, the family considered whether restructuring ownership — such as forming an LLC or establishing a trust — could streamline decision-making, improve tax benefits, or simplify things for family members in the future.

Pat described the immediate benefits of this process as "lifting a weight from our shoulders. Suddenly, we knew exactly where we stood legally, financially, and as a family. It made everything easier."

How Clear Ownership Empowers Your Family

Proactively confirming your ownership structure and title status provides several critical advantages for your family:

- **Less Stress:** Clearly defined ownership reduces surprises and minimizes family disagreements.
- **Faster Decisions:** Knowing exactly who must agree on important decisions allows transactions to proceed quickly and smoothly.
- **Better Outcomes:** Accurate titles and simplified ownership arrangements support effective estate planning, enhance tax efficiency, and facilitate smoother transitions across generations.
- **Stronger Relationships:** Removing uncertainty leads to open communication, reduced tension, and healthier family interactions.

PRACTICAL STEPS YOUR FAMILY CAN TAKE TODAY

Many families like Pat's use this simple, clear approach to gathering and organizing their farm's essential information. These five practical, proactive steps will give your family lasting clarity, stronger relationships, and empowered decision-making:

1. **Professional Appraisals:** Engage farm, land, and timber appraisers who understand local farmland values, productivity, infrastructure, and market trends.
2. **Clear Ownership Documentation:** Confirm and clearly document your farm's ownership structure and resolve any potential legal or title issues.
3. **Detailed Farm Records:** Organize clear records of expenses, income, and cash flow. Soil fertility, yield histories, management practices, infrastructure upgrades, timber values, harvest history, lease agreements, and tenant agreements are also key.

4. **Regular Family Meetings:** Do your best to commit to family meetings, sharing farm updates, financial details, and stewardship decisions. Each family member will feel included, informed, and respected.

5. **Engage Trusted Advisors:** Successful families work closely with experienced farmland advisors, estate attorneys, accountants, and those who clearly understand family values and goals.

If you think selling is the best option but you're not ready to start taking proactive steps to gather all the data needed to paint a clear picture of your farm's Foundation of Value, bring this short list of questions to your next family meeting and discuss each point openly, honestly, and carefully:

- Have we clearly documented our farm's financial performance, stewardship practices, and management history, even if we don't plan to sell soon?
- Are our lease agreements and management practices aligned clearly with our family's long-term goals and values?
- Are we creating regular, clear opportunities for open, respectful family discussions about our farm's future?

And most importantly, remember that you don't have to do this alone. The decision to sell your farm, even at its clearest, can still feel daunting and emotional. That's why it's so important to lean on trusted relationships and experienced advisors who truly understand both farmland and family dynamics. For some families, establishing an advisory board can be a valuable option that offers objective guidance, strategic direction, and emotional support to help navigate critical decisions with confidence. If your family is like most, you'll find strength, reassurance, and comfort in knowing that you have people in your corner who understand exactly where you are, what you value, and how to guide you thoughtfully toward decisions you'll never regret.

Pat's family discovered profound comfort and clarity in having advisors who understood their unique needs, emotional journey, and long-term goals. These relationships helped them prepare the farm for sale, and they helped them prepare their hearts, their family relationships, and their future.

Even when you know selling is the right decision, it doesn't mean it's easy. The decision carries weight because the land carries meaning. But done with intention, selling can be one of the most courageous and values-driven decisions a family makes. It can be a moment of honoring the past, securing the present, and freeing the future.

Whether your family decides to sell or stay, remember: Peace of mind is priceless, preparation is stewardship, and your family's true legacy is the values you carry forward.

Get the Support You Need

If you're ready to find the right partners to help you uncover the best path forward, I'd be honored to guide you through the process of identifying solutions that maximize your farm's value, honor your family's legacy, and lay the foundation for the vision you have for your future. With a wide range of personal and confidential advisory services, farmland partnerships, and unmatched industry expertise, my team and I are here to help your family farm become the next best version of itself.

Visit AmericanFamilyFarmland.com/work-with-johnny-klemme to get started.

CHAPTER 10

What's Next?

Pause for a moment.

Breathe.

You've done something remarkable.

You've walked through the emotions. Faced hard family conversations. Balanced financial realities with deeply rooted values. You've asked not only "What is this land worth?" but also "What does this land mean?"

Whether you're leaning toward keeping your farm or preparing to sell it, the insights you've gained have already transformed your perspective and are now your compass. Whatever path you've chosen, this chapter is your roadmap to ensure that your actions now reflect your values and vision.

NEXT STEPS IF YOU'RE KEEPING THE FARM

If your heart tells you that keeping the farm is your path forward, embrace that decision with confidence. It's a courageous and meaningful choice that says, "Our story continues here."

But it's important to remember that keeping the farm is an act of preservation and a commitment. A commitment to lead with intention, care for what's been entrusted to you, and align your personal goals with your broader purpose. Maybe your family will continue to farm the land yourselves. Maybe you'll hire a manager or lease it to a tenant. Whatever the case, your farm needs leadership. It needs vision. It needs someone willing to ask hard questions and make thoughtful plans. And that all starts by getting clear about what kind of future you want to build and who's helping you build it.

If your family is continuing to farm the land yourselves, you already know this is a way of life that demands more than early mornings and hard work. But even for seasoned producers, success today takes thoughtful planning, clear communication, and the ability to adapt. If you're the farming heir who's been carrying this for years, this is your chance to bring others into the conversation, share the realities, and help create a future that works for *everyone*.

And now that you've identified your core values and embraced the importance of Return on Life thinking, you recognize that real success involves more than financial returns alone. It's about how your investment in the farm supports your personal well-being, strengthens your family dynamics, and helps you achieve your long-term vision. True ROL, in this context, blends economic outcomes with emotional and relational rewards, ensuring your decisions enrich your life in ways far beyond the balance sheet.

Working toward holistic success might mean having honest conversations about who's handling finances, who's managing day-to-day operations, and who's helping navigate decisions about technology, conservation, or marketing. It could also mean admitting where you need help or identifying where old habits are getting in the way of growth.

It also means staying flexible. Agriculture today isn't the same as it was 10 or 20 years ago. Markets shift. Technology advances. Consumers evolve. You may have to do things differently than your parents or grandparents did. If you want the farm to thrive, you'll need to stay curious, open-minded, and willing to adapt.

And don't forget the human side of all this. Farms are notorious for blending work and home life to the point where boundaries disappear. But your family's health, peace, and relationships matter just as much as the next crop or livestock cycle. Because of this, it's crucial that you make time for rest and to protect your family's connection to each other.

Finally, if this is the path you've chosen, you must frequently revisit your succession plan and talk about the future with your immediate and extended family. Don't wait for a crisis to start preparing for what comes next. Keeping the farm is a beautiful decision, but you will only thrive when you lead with clarity, communicate with honesty, and protect the values you're trying to pass on.

Bringing in the Right Partner to Protect What Matters Most

Not every family has the time, expertise, or desire to manage day-to-day farm operations, and that's okay. In fact, choosing to bring in a professional farm manager can be one of the wisest, most values-driven decisions you make.

However, not all managers are the same. When I talk with families about this transition, I often remind them that the best farm managers don't just show up with spreadsheets or rent rates. Yes, you're looking for someone who knows the land. Someone with deep local knowledge of soil types, drainage, market conditions, and what makes tenant relationships work.

But you also want someone who will show up with curiosity, ask the right questions, and listen for what matters to *you*. They want to know what your family built, what your values are, and what kind of future you're trying to create.

When hiring a farm manager, your job is to find the right partner who understands that your land is more than a land asset. You'll know you've found the right person when they don't just talk about bushels, they talk about your goals and vision, listen to what matters to your family, and help translate that into smart operational decisions. When they treat your property like something they're *personally* invested in and proactively help you find new opportunities. If they can bring that mindset while also offering sound financial judgment, regular reporting, and a clear strategy for protecting your land's long-term value, you've found a rare and valuable partner.

And don't underestimate chemistry. You should feel like you can be honest with your manager and that they'll tell you the truth and represent you well when they're working with tenants or making big decisions. Because the farm may be in their hands, but your family's heritage is still your responsibility.

So, take your time. Ask questions. Trust your gut. The right farm manager helps protect everything your family has spent generations building and helps move it forward in a way that feels aligned with who you are.

NEXT STEPS IF YOU'RE SELLING THE FARM

If your family has made the difficult decision to sell the farm, I want you to know that you haven't failed and you're not giving up. You're doing something incredibly brave by deciding to move forward with honesty, clarity, diligence, and care. For some families, it's a decision rooted in emotion. For others, it's a matter of timing, strategy, or stewardship. Either way, it's valid and it deserves to be honored.

Now, the next step is choosing the right broker or advisor. This should be someone who understands pricing, contracts, and negotiation and who is also willing to be a partner — someone who listens, who asks the right questions, and who understands that this isn't just a transaction; it's your family's story. The best advisors bring both strategy and sensitivity. They show up with market data and a detailed analysis, yes, but also with the kind of presence that makes you feel understood.

So, how do you know when you've found the right advisor?

You'll feel it when they speak about farmland the way you do. You'll notice when they ask about your goals *before* they talk about pricing. You'll trust them because they're transparent, informed, and deeply respectful of your family dynamics. They'll bring experience *and* empathy. They'll offer strategy with sensitivity.

When you're ready to sit down with an advisor, the most important thing you can do is be organized and intentional. Start with clarity instead of struggling to achieve perfection. Gathering key documents ahead of time won't just make the meeting more productive; it will help your advisor understand what they're truly working with. It gives them the ability to offer better guidance, explore more strategic opportunities, and walk you through every step with confidence.

Still, you don't need to have all your documents perfectly assembled before your first meeting. What matters is that you're moving toward clarity and that you're open to the process. Bring any paperwork you have, including deeds, surveys, title reports, crop yields, fertility maps, lease agreements, notes about conservation work, financials (if you have them), and even handwritten notes that explain what's been done and why.

If something's missing? Don't worry. A good advisor will help you fill in the blanks. They'll ask the right questions to understand what's been done, what needs to happen, and how to move forward without missing critical details. They'll also help you uncover what really matters to you and how that shows up in the numbers, the lease terms, the boundaries, and the expectations you've quietly held onto for years.

And if you've never sold land before, it's easy to wonder if you're "doing it right." I often encourage clients to think of this experience like sharing a story instead of handing over a file. And like any good story, yours deserves to be told clearly, honestly, and with the kind of care that reflects just how much this land has meant to your family.

So, before you step into the first meeting with an advisor, ask yourself:

- What story do I want this sale to tell?
- What do I hope the outcome will feel like financially and emotionally?
- What questions have I been afraid to ask, and who could help me finally ask them?

Remember, this isn't a test; it's a conversation. And the more you bring to the table, the more your advisor can serve you well.

MOVING FORWARD WITH STRENGTH, CONFIDENCE, AND HEART

You've thoughtfully considered the emotions, strategy, stewardship, and practical steps of selling your family farm. You've explored how your farm can align with your life's deepest goals. And now, you have the clarity, practical guidance, and emotional tools to make decisions you'll be proud of.

Generations before you have stood in this same space and wondered what the right decision looks like. You're not the first to feel the weight of your family's history or the pull of change. But you are among the few who've chosen to face it with honesty, wisdom, and purpose.

So, gather your family around the kitchen table one more time. Share what you've learned. Listen carefully and openly to each other. And remember that you don't have to have all the answers right away. You just have to begin with care, clarity, and courage. Whether you sell this year, next year, or never at all, know this: You are not walking away; you are walking *toward* the life you've worked so hard to build.

So, what's your next best step?

Start with a conversation.

Start with your values.

Start with your goals.

Start with the people around your table.

Start with a vision grounded in the LAND VALUES framework so your decisions reflect who you are and what you care about most.

You don't have to navigate this alone. I'm here to help you move from uncertainty to the future you've been hoping for.

The Next Chapter Is Yours to Write

I ran into Pat last spring at the local farm supply store, of all places. I barely recognized him at first. His smile was broad and relaxed, and there was a brightness in his eyes that hadn't been there when we first met.

We stood by a seed display next to some toy tractors, talking easily and catching up.

"You know," he said, nodding toward his grandkids running between the aisles, "this wasn't an easy decision at first. Letting go of the farm felt like we were losing a piece of ourselves. But the truth is, we gained so much more."

His gaze softened. "We sleep easier. We enjoy life more. And honestly? The family is closer now than we've been in decades. I've never regretted it for a second."

He paused, reflecting. Then, he smiled again. "Selling gave us space — space to breathe, space to reconnect, space to focus on each other. It didn't erase everything overnight, but it helped lift the pressure and gave us a fresh start. The kids are thriving.

Jenny and I finally took that trip we'd always talked about. And in a way, that freedom helped us honor our past by finally letting go of what was holding us back."

Not long after my encounter with Pat, I got a call from Emily Taylor.

It had been a few years since her family chose to transform their farm. Her voice carried a sense of calm confidence as she described the life they'd created, which now included a thriving wedding venue, specialty crops growing strong, and her kids finishing up chores before heading off to 4-H meetings.

"We almost sold," she admitted. Her voice cracked slightly, like the memory had caught her off guard. "I'm so glad we redefined what the farm meant to us. Now, it's about community, sustainability, and family. It's still hard work — and there are days we wonder if we're doing it right — but it's deeply rewarding. Keeping the farm didn't solve everything, but it gave us a renewed sense of purpose that we hold on to every single day."

"I'm glad to hear you're so happy," I told her. "I know things got tough there for a while."

"It wasn't easy," she said. "There were times we wondered if we'd made a mistake. But looking back now, our return has been richer than we ever imagined. The farm isn't just surviving — it's thriving. And it's ours in a way it never could have been before."

THE RIGHT PATH IS UNIQUE TO YOU

Pat's family chose to sell. The Taylors chose to reimagine. Two different outcomes rooted in the same truth. Both families aligned their decisions with their values. They led with clear confidence, not confusion. They let their story be about the land

and the life they wanted to live. And that's what your journey, as you've read this book, has been about, too.

You've walked through stories, memories, and emotions that stretch far beyond soil, creeks, the woods edge, and acreage. You've deepened your understanding, navigated complexity, and chosen to live with purpose. And whether you're passing the land on, managing it yourself, hiring someone to help, or preparing to sell, you now hold something incredibly valuable.

You now have more than a plan and a language to protect your legacy. You have a fresh understanding and perhaps a clear vision of what your family's Return on Life can really look like. You have a renewed sense of what your land — and your life — can really mean.

Your next chapter may involve fields, livestock, family meetings, leases, or even letting go, but whatever it looks like, you'll move forward with intention and purpose.

That next chapter? It's yours to write. And I hope that one day I'll get to hear about the legacy you've created.

So, whether your next step is planning, selling, or simply gathering your family around the kitchen table to discuss the next growing season, it's time to begin. Take the first step. This is your land, your legacy, and your life.

Thank You

To the families I've served, thank you for letting me sit at your tables, walk your fields, rest under your trees, play in your creeks, and listen to your stories. Your courage to face hard decisions, your willingness to be vulnerable, and your commitment to your land and legacy have inspired every page.

To my colleagues and team, you've sharpened my thinking, challenged me to grow, and shown what it means to work with excellence and purpose. Thank you for believing in this message and standing beside me.

To the mentors who believed in me, thank you for your wisdom, honesty, and willingness to walk ahead so that I could follow sure-footedly. I hope this book reflects a fraction of what you've poured into me.

To my friends and peers who do this important work, you are the quiet backbone of so many stories. I see your dedication, your long days, your heart for both land and people. Keep going — we're doing something that matters.

To my family, my anchor. You've made sacrifices, cheered me on, and reminded me what's worth protecting. Thank you for keeping me grounded.

And to the reader holding this book, thank you. For showing up. For caring about your story. For choosing to lead with love and legacy. My hope is that this work has helped you find answers, your voice, your purpose, and your next best step.

With deep gratitude,
Johnny Klemme

About the Author

Johnny Klemme is widely recognized and respected as an expert advisor, farmland broker, and auctioneer with extensive experience in farmland real estate transactions across the Midwest. His reputation in the agricultural community is built upon decades of professionalism and a genuine dedication to serving farm families and rural communities.

Having personally been affected by the sale of his own family's farmland, Johnny provides a genuine, empathetic perspective that many farmland owners immediately recognize and connect with. He speaks not just as an advisor but as someone who has walked the journey.

Clients consistently highlight Johnny's strong communication skills, empathetic approach, and unwavering dedication to their best interests. His deep understanding of family dynamics, personal farmland experience, and clear, strategic advice has established him as both a trusted advisor and thought leader in farmland ownership and legacy transitions.

CONTACT

AmericanFamilyFarmland.com
LandValues.com
GFarmland.com

www.ingramcontent.com/pod-product-compliance
Lightning Source LLC
Chambersburg PA
CBHW071214210326
41597CB00016B/1813